John Raymond Howard

Educational Nuggets

Plato, Aristotle, Rousseau, Herbart, Spencer, Harris, Butler, Eliot

John Raymond Howard

Educational Nuggets
Plato, Aristotle, Rousseau, Herbart, Spencer, Harris, Butler, Eliot

ISBN/EAN: 9783337102791

Printed in Europe, USA, Canada, Australia, Japan

Cover: Foto ©Thomas Meinert / pixelio.de

More available books at **www.hansebooks.com**

Educational Nuggets

PLATO ARISTOTLE ROUSSEAU HERBART
SPENCER HARRIS BUTLER ELIOT

Gathered by JOHN R. HOWARD

NEW YORK:
FORDS, HOWARD, & HULBERT

NOTE.

THE aim of this little group of discon-
nected yet closely related paragraphs on
Education is suggestiveness, inspiration, and
encouragement,—and that especially for the
training of right-minded men and women
as citizens of our American republic.

Systems of Education have been many
and various, each suited to its time; yet
from Plato's day to our own the finest minds
have seen in it all a lofty unity, which in the
present age is developing into a scientific
method, based on the study of nature, man,
and society. " Consistency and universality
are the tests of truth," says Professor Jowett; and in the best ideals of Education
these tests hold, from ancient Greece to
modern America.

Happily the spirit of our time, in the
earnest consideration of Education as a
science, is diffusing this larger conception
more and more widely. Yet many teachers

rebel against the social order of his time—
wrought damage with his political writings,
but was a prophet of blessing to all children.
The tender, patient study of childhood,
taught in his *Émile*, inspired the new epoch
in Education which has signalized the present century. It was the direct stimulus of
Pestalozzi, who brought the ideas of spon-
taneity and self-activity into practical educational work, and of his disciple Froebel, the
originator of the Kindergarten with all its
suggestive principles. Avoiding a tempta-
tion to interesting details, the compilation
omits these two reformers. The one following Rousseau is Herbart, whose psychology
informs all the educational science of our
day. Spencer—the great co-ordinator of all
sciences under the general principles of the
evolutionary doctrine—that marvel of special knowledges and of almost universal wisdom in arraying them—is represented by
pregnant paragraphs from his treatise on
Education.

After Spencer come three men in active
American life to-day. These are : Harris—
whose writings are standard, and whose

labors as United States Commissioner of Education have done much towards unifying our American school systems; Butler— whose original impetus to the Teachers' College, and whose helpful interest in our common schools, despite his special work in the chair of Philosophy at Columbia, are felt throughout the land; and Eliot—the masterly head of Harvard, the chief apostle of the elective courses, whose educational ideas embrace a harmonious progress from Kindergarten to University.

From these thoughtful students of the science and practical experts in the art of Education, parents, teachers, and those who are likely to become such, can draw many suggestions of value. The few extracts gathered from their writings will, it is hoped, inspire the wish to know more of them. In every case the title, author, and publisher of volumes quoted from have been named, not only in recognition of courteous permissions to make extracts but in the hope that these briefs from living books will interest readers to draw more fully from the original sources, and to read the books themselves.

CONTENTS.

PLATO.

"Out of Plato come all things that are still written and debated among men of thought. Great havoc makes he among our originalities. We have reached the mountain from which all these drift bowlders were detached."—*Emerson.*

FROM "THE REPUBLIC."[1]

A STATE arises out of the needs of mankind; no one is self-sufficing, but all of us have many wants. . . . Then as we have many wants, and many persons are needed to supply them, one takes a helper for one purpose and another for another: and when these partners and helpers are gathered together in one habitation, the body of inhabitants is termed a State.

He who is to be a really good and noble guardian of the State will require to unite in himself philosophy and spirit and swiftness and strength.

---

[1] THE DIALOGUES OF PLATO. Translation of B. JOWETT. Oxford : Clarendon Press, 1875.

Then we have found the desired natures : and now that we have found them how are they to be reared and educated ? [1]

Can we find a better than the traditional sort ?—and this has two divisions, gymnastic for the body and music for the soul.

And when you speak of music, do you include literature or not ?—I do.

And literature may be either true or false. And the young should be trained in both kinds, and we begin with the false. . . . We begin by telling children stories, which, though not wholly destitute of truth, are in the main fictitious.

You know also that the beginning is the most important part of any work, especially in the case of a young and tender thing :

---

[1] " No pains are spared in Europe to educate princes and nobles who are to govern. No expense is counted too great to prepare the governing classes for their function. America has her governing class too ; and that governing class is the whole people."—H. W. BEECHER.

for that is the time at which the character is being formed and the desired impression is more readily taken.

A young person cannot judge what is allegorical and what is literal ; anything that he receives into his mind at that age is likely to become indelible and unalterable ; and therefore it is most important that the tales which the young first hear should be models of virtuous thought.

Beauty of style and harmony and grace and good rhythm depend on simplicity,—I mean the simplicity of a rightly and nobly ordered character. . . . And ugliness and discord and inharmonious motion are nearly allied to ill words and ill nature, as grace and harmony are the twin sisters of goodness and virtue, and bear their image.

We would not have our guardians grow up amid images of moral deformity, as in some noxious pasture, and then browse and feed upon many a baneful herb and flower day by day, little by little, until they silently gather a festering mass of corruption in their own soul. Let our artists rather be those who are gifted to discern the true nature of the beautiful and graceful ; then will our youth dwell in a land of health, amid fair sights and sounds, and receive the good in everything; and beauty, the effluence of fair works, shall flow into the eye and ear, like a health-giving breeze from a purer region, and insensibly draw the soul from earliest years into likeness and sympathy with the beauty of reason.

And, therefore, musical [including literary] training is a more potent instrument than any other, because rhythm and harmony find their way into the inward places of the soul, on which they mightily fasten, imparting grace, and making the soul of him who is rightly educated graceful or of him who is ill-educated ungraceful ; and also because he who has received this true education of the inner being will most shrewdly perceive omissions or faults in art and nature, and with a true taste, while he praises and rejoices over and receives into his soul the good, and becomes noble and good, he will justly blame and hate the bad, now, in the days of his youth, even before he is able to know the reason why; and when reason comes he will recognize and salute the friend with whom his education has made him long familiar.

And when a beautiful soul harmonizes with a beautiful form, and the two are cast in one mould, that will be the fairest of sights to him who has an eye to see it.

Gymnastic as well as music should begin in early years; the training in it should be careful and should continue through life. Now my belief is not that the good body by any bodily excellence improves the soul, but, on the contrary, that the good soul, by her own excellence, improves the body as far as this may be possible.

The very exercises and toils which he undergoes are intended to stimulate the spirited element of his nature, and not to increase his strength; he will not, like common athletes, use exercise and regimen to develop his muscles. Neither are the two arts of music and gymnastic really designed, as is often supposed, the one for the training of the soul, the other for the training of the body. The teachers of both have in view chiefly the improvement of the soul.

Did you never observe the effect on the mind itself of exclusive devotion to gymnastic, or the opposite effect of an exclusive devotion to music ? The one produces a temper of hardness and ferocity, the other of softness and effeminacy. . . . And as there are two principles of human nature, one the spirited [that of forceful energy] and the other the philosophical [that of thought and reason], some God, as I should say, has given mankind two arts answering to them (and only indirectly to the soul and body) in order that these two principles (like the strings of an instrument) may be relaxed or drawn tighter until they are harmonized.

And he who mingles music with gymnastic in the fairest proportions, and best attempers them to the soul, may be rightly called the true musician or harmonist in a far higher sense than the tuner of the strings. And such a presiding genius will always be required in our State, if the government is to last.

The State if once started well moves with accumulating force like a wheel. For good nurture and education emplant good constitutions, and these good constitutions taking root in a good education improve more and more, and their improvement affects the breed in men as in other animals.

When they have by the help of music gained the spirit of good order, then this habit of order will accompany them in all their actions and be a principle of growth to them, and if there are any fallen places in the State will raise them up again.

Of course they will go on expeditions together; and will take with them any children who are strong enough, that, after the manner of the artisan's child, they may look on at the

the business of later life, and should be for the most part imitations of the occupations which they will hereafter pursue in earnest.

Youth should be kept strangers to all that is bad, and especially to things which suggest vice or hate.

There are two periods of life into which education has to be divided, from seven to the age of puberty, and onwards to the age of one-and-twenty.

The neglect of education does harm to states.

The citizen should be moulded to suit the government under which he lives.

That education should be regulated by law and should be an affair of state is not to be denied.

There can be no doubt that children should be taught those useful things which are really necessary, but not all things ; for occupations are divided into liberal and illiberal, and to young children should be imparted only such

This is knowledge of the kind for which we are seeking, having a double use, military and philosophical ; for the man of war must learn the art of numbers or he will not know how to array his troops, and the philosopher also, because he has to arise out of the sea of change and lay hold of true being, and therefore he must be an arithmetician. . . . We must endeavor to persuade those who are to be the principal men of our State to go and learn *Arithmetic*, not as amateurs, but they must carry on the study until they see the nature of numbers with the mind only. . . . Arithmetic has a very great and elevating effect, compelling the mind to reason about abstract number.

And have you further observed that those who have a natural talent for calculation are generally quick at every other kind of knowledge ; and even the dull, if they have had an arithmetical training, although they may derive no other advantage from it, always become much quicker than they otherwise would have been. . . . And for all these reasons arithmetic is a kind of knowledge in which the best natures should be trained.

For that part of the kindred science [*Geometry*] which related to war a very little of either geometry or calculation will be enough ; the question relates rather to the greater and more advanced part of geometry —whether that tends in any degree to make more easy the vision of the idea of good. . . . The knowledge at which geometry aims is knowledge of the eternal, and not of aught perishing or transient. . . . Geometry will draw the soul towards the truth and create the spirit of philosophy.

And suppose we make *Astronomy* the third—what do you say ?

I am strongly inclined to it, he said ; the observation of the seasons and of weather and years is as essential to the general as it is to the farmer and sailor.

I am amused, I said, at your fear of the world which makes you guard against the appearance of insisting upon useless studies ; I quite admit the difficulty of believing that

in every man there is an eye of the soul
which, when by other pursuits lost and
dimmed, is by these purified and re-illu-
mined; and is more precious far than ten
thousand bodily eyes, for by it alone is truth
seen. . . . And will not a true astronomer
have the same feeling when he looks at the
movements of the stars ? Will he not think
that heaven and the things in heaven are
framed by the Creator of them in the most
perfect manner ?

The teachers of *Harmony* compare the
sounds and consonances which are heard
only, and their labor, like that of the astronomer, is in vain. . . . They investigate the
numbers of the harmonies which are heard,
but they never attain to problems—that is to
say, they never reach the natural harmonies of
numbers, or reflect why some numbers are
harmonious and others not. . . . A thing
which I would call useful; that is, if sought
after with a view to the beautiful and good ;
but if pursued in any other spirit, useless.

And so we have at last arrived at the

hymn of *Dialectic* [Philosophy]. This is of that strain which is of the intellect only. . . . this power of elevating the highest principle in the soul to the contemplation of that which is best in existence—this power is given by all that study and pursuit of the arts which has been described. . . . Dialectic, then, is the coping-stone of the sciences, and set over them ; no other science can be placed higher—the nature of knowledge can no further go.

Wherefore my counsel is, that we hold fast ever to the heavenly way and follow after justice and virtue always, considering that the soul is immortal and able to endure every sort of good and every sort of evil. Thus shall we live dear to one another and to the gods, both while remaining here and when, like conquerors in the games who go round to gather gifts, we receive our reward. And it shall be well with us, both in this life and in the pilgrimage of a thousand years.

ARISTOTLE.

" The great master of all the peculiarities of nature and of men, the eager investigator . . . . the mighty Aristotle."—EWALD.

FROM " THE POLITICS."[1]

MEN must engage in business and go to war, but leisure and peace are better ; they must do what is necessary and useful, but what is honorable is better. In such principles children and persons of every age which requires education should be trained.

In men reason and mind are the end towards which nature strives, so that the birth and moral discipline of the citizens ought to be ordered with a view to them.

The directors of education, as they are termed, should be careful what tales or stories the children hear, for the sports of children are designed to prepare the way for

---

[1] THE POLITICS. Translated by B. JOWETT. Oxford ; Clarendon Press, 1885.

work which they will have to do when they are grown up. . . . Did you never observe in the arts how the potter's boys look on and help long before they touch the wheel?

The power and capacity of learning exists in the soul already; and, just as the eye is unable to turn from darkness to light without the whole body, so too the instrument of knowledge can only by the movement of the whole soul be turned from the world of becoming into that of being, and learn by degrees to endure the sight of being, and of the brightest and best of being, or in other words, of the good.

What sort of knowledge is there which would draw the soul from becoming to being? . . . . We shall have to take something which is not special but of universal application; a something which all arts, sciences and intelligences use in common, and which every one first has to learn among the elements of education—the little matter of distinguishing one, two, or three— in a word, number and calculation. . . .

kinds of knowledge as will be useful to them without vulgarizing them. And any occupation, art, or science, which makes the body or soul or mind of the freeman less fit for the practice or exercise of virtue, is vulgar.

To be always seeking after the useful does not become free and exalted souls.

Two principles have to be kept in view, what is possible, what is becoming : at these every man ought to aim.

Education should be based upon three principles—the Mean [moderate], the Possible, the Becoming [decorous], these three.

JEAN JACQUES ROUSSEAU

" The spirit of education which fills and animates the work has shaken to their foundations and purified all the school rooms, and even the nurseries, in Europe."—JEAN PAUL FRIEDERICH RICHTER.

FROM " ÉMILE."[1]

Introduction by the Translator.

IN education, there have been recurring periods when some partial thought has secured such domination that wholesome training has become impossible, till a reformer appears who restores the lost equilibrium, and then very likely he inaugurates a movement which leads up to another catastrophe.

At times education becomes almost wholly "livresque," devoted to the study of books and words rather than of things, and at

---

[1] ROUSSEAU'S ÉMILE ; OR TREATISE ON EDUCATION. Abridged, Translated, and Annotated by WILLIAM H. PAYNE, Ph.D., L.L.D. A volume in " The International Education Series." New York : D. APPLETON & CO. 1895.

others it becomes mainly literary or humanis-
tic, to the neglect of the study of matter.

The records of human thought, sentiment
and achievement form one term of the contrast, while matter and its phenomena, under
the term Nature, constitute the other.
Ever since education began to have a history human thought has oscillated with
almost rhythmical movement from one of
these poles to the other, but with a general
tendency toward the study of letters ; and
so it has usually happened that educational
reform has invited a return to Nature, and
has sounded a warning against books and
words.

Let us make a summary analysis of the
education that Rousseau would have substituted for that which he covers with his con-
demnation. . . .

I. *Education should be natural.* . . .
A return to Nature is a return to simplicity.
There is much truth in Rousseau's saying,

that we no longer know how to be simple
in anything. Look at the countless devices
and machines for teaching a child how to
read! What useless lumber! Create in the
child a desire to read, and all this apparatus
is of no account ; the process becomes sim-
plified to the last degree, and the child cannot be held back from learning how to read.

To follow Nature also signifies to return
to reality. There may be formal teaching
just as there is formal logic, both arts being
occupied with symbols and not with reali-
ties. The universal teaching instrument is
language, and the use of symbols is unavoidable, but teacher and pupil should understand that these symbols must be vitalized
by a content.

To follow Nature is to resort to personal
experience rather than to follow authority ;
it is to gain knowledge at first hand rather
than to accept the results of other men's experience. As Rousseau puts it in a concrete way, " The child is not to learn science,
but to discover it." This is akin to the

dogma of Socrates, "Science can not be taught, only drawn out." This doctrine has been pushed to its furthest limit by Mr. Spencer, who makes education consist in the process of rediscovery, and requires each child to reproduce the experiences of the race.

To trust to mere authority altogether is absurd ; it is to forego the pleasure of living, and in an important sense to cease to be a man : but to renounce authority altogether, and to depend for our knowledge wholly on our own experience, is simply impossible, and if possible, would be very absurd. There is evidently a middle ground which leaves a wide field for personal experience, and at the same time allows the individual to give almost indefinite extension to his knowledge by appropriating the accumulated experiences of the race.

Simplify your methods as much as possible ; distrust the artificial aids that complicate the process of learning ; bring your pupil face to face with reality ; connect symbol with substance ; make learning, so

far as possible, a process of personal discovery ; depend as little as possible on mere
authority. This is my interpretation of
Rousseau's precept, " Follow Nature."

II. *Education should be progressive*—
The mind, like the body, passes through
successive stages of growth, and in both
cases the transition from one stage to the
next indicates a corresponding change in
treatment. . . . Infancy is a little world so
peculiar in nature and need as to be virtually
cut off from the succeeding stage of life,
and hence requires a treatment peculiarly
its own. . . . The next section of human
life is childhood. The child has his peculiar
nature and needs ; the treatment due an
infant must be abandoned, and a new
system adopted in conformity with the
nature of this new creature.

Boyhood follows childhood, and manhood,
in turn, succeeds boyhood. These are successive, and in some sense independent, sections of human life, and so peculiar in nature
and need as to require modes of treatment
specifically different.

This, in outline, is Rousseau's theory of progressive education. The obvious thing to be said of it is that it is so systematic and artificial as to be unnatural.

Education should be progressive in the same sense and to the same degree that life and growth are progressive ; not progressive in the sense of an abrupt winding up of a lower system of regimen and an equally abrupt inauguration of a higher, but progressive in the actual wholesome sense of insensible ascent and modification.

III. *Education should be negative. . . .* Rousseau believed that as education was administered in the schools of his day there was a vast disproportion between the mass of knowledge accumulated and the child's power to comprehend and use it ; and so, in his usual aphoristic style, he says that the important thing in education is not to gain time, but to lose it, and that he would prefer that Émile should reach his twelfth year without knowing his right hand from his left, or right from wrong.

Here as elsewhere we shall fail in our interpretation of Rousseau if we do more or less than catch the general spirit of his paradox.

If, in imitation of Rousseau, I were to try my hand at a paradox, I would say, in this connection, that useless knowledge is sometimes the most useful; meaning by this that the subjects that are best for pure training are sometimes of the least value for practical purposes. Algebra and geometry are instances of this; they are incomparable disciplines, but the average student derives only very little advantage from the knowledge that is acquired while the discipline is in progress.

Again, by making education negative, or, as Rousseau says to the same purpose, by losing time rather than by trying to gain it, we extend the period of childhood and allow the pupil to lead a sort of vegetative life, which Froebel seems to have had in mind when he conceived the occupations and gifts at the kindergarten.

The *Émile* has justly been called the Gospel of Childhood. If it had no other claims to consideration it would deserve the homage of parents and teachers by reason of that sacredness with which it invests the personality of every child. In what other book of human origin can we find such compassion for the weakness of childhood, such tender regard for its happiness, and such touching pleas for its protection and guidance? What other book has ever recalled mothers to a sense of their duties with such pathos and effect? The *Émile* has made the ministry of the school-room as sacred as the ministry of the altar; and by unfolding the mysteries of his art and disclosing the secret of his power, it has made the teacher's office one of honor and respect.

The power of the book lies in its general spirit rather than in any doctrine or method which it embodies. If read with kindly feeling and without prejudice, it cannot fail to inspire teachers with the noblest ambition, and to quicken their methods with living power.

ÉMILE.

Author's Preface.

We do not know childhood. Acting on the false ideas we have of it, the farther we go the farther we wander from the right path. Those who are wisest are attached to what is important for men to know, without considering what children are able to apprehend. They are always looking for the man in the child, without thinking of what he was before he became a man. . . . Begin, then, by studying your pupils more thoroughly, for it is very certain that you do not know them.

Infancy—General Principles.

People pity the lot of a child ; they do not see that the human race would have perished if man had not begun by being a child.

We are born weak; we have need of strength : we are born stupid ; we have need of judgment. All that we have not at our birth, but which we need when we are grown, is given us by education.

The natural man is complete in himself; he is the numerical unit, the absolute whole, who is related only to himself or to his fellow-man. Civilized man is but a fractional unit that is dependent upon its denominator, and whose value consists in its relation to the whole, which is the social organization.

What would a man be worth for others who had been educated solely for himself?

In the natural order of things, all men being equal, their common vocation is manhood, and whoever is well trained for that cannot fulfill badly any vocation connected with it. Whether my pupil be destined for the army, the church, or the bar, concerns me but little. Regardless of the vocation of his parents, nature summons him to the duties of human life. To live, is the trade I wish to teach him.

Ever since mothers, despising their first duty, have been no longer willing to nourish their own children, they must be entrusted to hireling nurses, who, thus finding themselves mothers to others' children for whom the voice of nature did not plead, have felt no anxiety but to rid themselves of their burdens.

Where there is no mother there can be no child. Their duties are reciprocal; and if they are badly fulfilled on one side, they will be neglected on the other.

But a woman may miss the right way by taking an opposite course: when, instead of neglecting her motherly duties, she carries them to an extreme; when she makes of her child her idol; when she augments and nourishes his weakness in order to prevent him from feeling it.

Observe Nature, and follow the route which she traces for you. . . . She is ever exciting children to activity; she hardens the constitution by trials of every sort.

Experience shows that there are more deaths among children delicately reared

than among others.   Provided the strength
of children is not overtaxed, there is less
risk in using it than in preventing its use.

A father who merely feeds and clothes
the children he has begotten so far fulfills
but a third of his task.   To the race, he
owes men ; to society, men of social disposi-
tions ; and to the state, citizens.   Every
man who can pay this triple debt and does
not pay it, is guilty of a crime, and the
more guilty, perhaps, when the debt is only
half paid.   He who can not fulfill the duties
of a father has no right to become such.

Men were not made to be massed together
in herds, but to be scattered over the earth
which they are to cultivate.   The more they
herd together the more they corrupt one
another. . . . The breath of man is fatal to
his fellows ; this is no less true literally than
figuratively.

Cities are the graves of the human species.
After a few generations, races perish or
degenerate ; they must be renewed, and this
regeneration is always supplied by the coun-

try. Send your children away, therefore, so that they may renew themselves, so to speak, and regain, amid the fields, the vigor they have lost in the unwholesome air of places too thickly peopled.

The education of man begins at his birth. Before he can speak, before he can understand, he is already instructing himself. Experience precedes lessons; the moment he knows his nurse he has already acquired much knowledge. We should be surprised at the knowledge possessed by the most boorish man, if we followed his progress from the moment of birth to the present hour of his life. If we were to divide all human knowledge into two parts, one common to all men and the other restricted to scholars, the last would be very small compared with the first.

When a child weeps he is in a state of discomfort; he has some need which he can not satisfy. We look about in search of this need, and when we have found it provide for it.

The first tears of children are prayers, and
unless we are on our guard they soon become orders. Children begin by being
assisted, but end by being served. . . . And
already we begin to see why, in this early
period of life, it is important to discern the
secret intention which dictates the gesture
or the cry.

A child wishes to disarrange whatever he
sees; he breaks and injures whatever he can
reach; he seizes a bird as he would a stone,
and strangles it without knowing what he
does. . . . Whether he makes or unmakes
matters not; it suffices that he changes the
state of things, and every change is an
action. Though he seems to have a greater
inclination to destroy, this is not through
badness. The activity which forms is always slow; and as that which destroys is
more rapid, it is better adapted to his vivac-
ity.

From the Age of Five to Twelve.

It is through the sensible effects of signs
that children judge of their meaning; for

them, there is no other convention. Whatever ill may befall the child, it is very rare that he cries when he is alone, at least if he has no hope of being heard.

If he falls and bumps his head, if his nose bleeds, or if he cuts his fingers, instead of rushing to him with an air of alarm, I remain unmoved, at least for a little time. . . . In reality it is not so much the cut, but the fear, which torments him when he is wounded. I will at least spare him this last suffering; for most certainly he will judge of his misfortune as he sees that I judge of it.

As children grow in strength, complaining is less necessary for them. . . . Along with their growth in power there is developed the knowledge which puts them in a condition to direct it. It is at this second stage that the life of the individual properly begins. It is then that he takes knowledge of himself. Memory diffuses the feeling of identity over all the moments of his existence. He becomes truly one, the same, and consequently already capable of happiness or misery. It is important, then, that we begin to consider him here as a moral being.

Love childhood ; encourage its sports, its pleasures, its amiable instincts. Who of you has not sometimes looked back with regret on that age when a smile was ever on the lips, when the soul was ever at peace ? Why would you take from those little innocents the enjoyment of a time so short which is slipping from them, and of a good so precious which they can not abuse?

When he can ask for what he wants in words, and when, in order to obtain it more quickly, or to overcome a refusal, he supplements his demands with tears, it ought to be firmly refused him.

It is important always to grant at the first intimation what we do not mean to refuse.

Childhood has its own way of seeing, thinking, and feeling, and nothing is more foolish than to try to substitute our own for them. I would as soon require a child to be five feet in height as to have judgment at the age of ten.

Whatever you allow him to do, allow him to do it at the first suggestion, without solicitation, especially without entreaty and without conditions. Give your assent with cheerfulness, and never refuse save with reluctance ; but let all your refusals be irrevocable.

Punishment must never be inflicted on children as a punishment, but it ought always to come to them as the natural consequence of their bad acts.

Rattle-headed children become commonplace men. I know of no observation more general and more certain than this. Nothing is more difficult than to distinguish, in infancy, real stupidity from that apparent and deceptive stupidity which is the indication of strong characters. . . . During his infancy the younger Cato seemed an imbecile in the family. He was taciturn and obstinate, and this was all the judgment that

was formed of him. . . . Oh, how liable to
be deceived are they who are so precipitate
in their judgments of children ! . . . . Respect childhood, and do not hastily judge of
it either for good or for evil. Allow a long
time for the exceptions to be manifested,
proved, and confirmed, before adopting
special methods for them. Allow Nature to
act in her place, for fear of thwarting her
operations.

The apparent facility with which children
learn is the cause of their ruin. We do not
see that this very facility is the proof that
they are learning nothing. Their smooth
and polished brain reflects like a mirror
the objects that are presented to it ; but nothing remains, nothing penetrates it.

If Nature gives to a child's brain that plas-
ticity which renders it capable of receiving
all sorts of impressions, it is not for the purpose of engraving upon it the names of kings,
dates, terms in heraldry, astronomy, and
geography, and all those words without any
meaning for his age, and without any utility

for any age whatever, with which his sad and barren infancy is harassed ; but it is in order that all the ideas which he can conceive and which are useful to him, all those which relate to his happiness, and are one day to enlighten him as to his duties, may be traced there at an early hour in ineffaceable characters, and may serve him for self-conduct during his whole life in a manner adapted to his being and to his faculties.

To exercise the senses is not merely to make use of them, but it is to learn how to judge by them ; and it is also, so to speak, to learn how to feel, for we neither know how to touch, nor to see, nor to hear, save as we have been taught.

Do not exercise the child's strength alone, but call into exercise all the senses which direct it. Draw from each of them all the advantage possible, and then employ one to verify the impression made by another. Measure, count, weigh, compare, and do not employ force till after having estimated the resistance.

Do not reason with one whom you would cure of the horror of darkness; but take him often into dark places, and you may be sure that this practice is worth more than all the arguments of philosophy. Tilers on roofs do not become dizzy, and no one who is accustomed to being in darkness is any longer afraid of it.

Nothing is so cheerful as darkness. Never shut up your child in a black hole. Let him laugh as he goes into the darkness, and let him laugh again when he comes out of it.

Children, who are great imitators, all try their hand at drawing. I would have my pupil cultivate this art, not exactly for the art itself, but for rendering the eye accurate and the hand flexible. . . . He shall have no master but Nature, and no models but objects. He shall have before his eyes the very original, and not the paper which represents it ; he shall draw a house from a house, a tree from a tree, a man from a man. . . . I shall discourage him even from tracing anything from memory in the absence of objects, until, by frequent observations, their exact figures are firmly impressed on his imagination : for fear that, substituting odd and fantastic forms for the truth of things, he lose the knowledge of proportions and the taste for all the beauties of Nature.

From Twelve to Fifteen.

Although the whole course of life up to adolescence is a period of weakness, there is a point in the course of this first stage of life when, growth in power having surpassed the growth of needs, the growing animal, still absolutely weak, becomes relatively strong. All his needs not being developed, his actual powers are more than sufficient to provide for those which he has. As a man he would be very weak, but as a child he is very strong.

He whose strength exceeds his desires has some power to spare ; he is certainly a very strong being. This is the third stage of childhood, and the one of which I have now to speak.

At first, children are merely restless, then they are curious; and this curiosity, well directed, is the motive power of the age which we have now reached.

Make your pupil attentive to natural phenomena, and you will soon make him curious: . . . . In your search for the laws of Nature, always begin with the most common and the most obvious phenomena, and accustom your pupil not to take these phenomena for reasons, but for facts.

As soon as he comes to have sufficient knowledge of himself to conceive in what his welfare consists, as soon as he can grasp relations sufficiently to judge of what is best and what is not best for him, from that moment he is in a condition to feel the difference between work and play, and to regard the second merely as a respite from the first. Then objects of real utility may enter into his studies, and may invite him to give to them a more constant application than he gave to simple amusements.

The law of necessity, always reappearing,

teaches man from an early hour to do what does not please him, in order to prevent an evil which would be more displeasing. Such is the use of foresight; and from this foresight, well or badly regulated, springs all human wisdom or all human misery.

As soon as we succeeded in giving our pupil an idea of the word *useful*, we have another strong hold for governing him ; for this word makes a strong impression on him, provided he has only an idea of it in proportion to his age, and clearly sees how it is related to his actual welfare. . . . *What is this good for ?* Henceforth this is the consecrated word, the decisive word between him and me in all the transactions of our life.

When one has been taught, as his most important lesson, to desire nothing in the way of knowledge save what is useful, he asks questions like Socrates ; he does not ask a question without framing for himself its answer, which he knows will be demanded of him before resolving it.

To render a young man judicious, we must carefully form his judgments instead of dictating to him our own.

The art of the teacher consists in never allowing his observations to bear on minutiæ which serve no purpose, but ever to confront the child with the wide relations which he must one day know in order to judge correctly of the order, good and bad, of civil society.

Outside of society, an isolated man, owing nothing to any one, has a right to live as he pleases ; but in society, where he necessarily lives at the expense of others, he owes them in labor the price of his support ; to this there is no exception. To work, then, is a duty indispensable to social man. Rich or poor, powerful or weak, every idle citizen is a knave.

By causing to pass in review before a child the productions of Nature and art, by stimulating his curiosity and following it where it leads, we have the advantage of studying his tastes, his inclinations, and his propensities, and to see glitter the first spark of his genius, if he has genius of any decided sort.

But a common error, and one from which we must preserve ourselves, is to attribute to the ardor of talent the effect of the occasion, and to take for a marked inclination toward such or such an art the imitative spirit which is common to man and monkey, and which mechanically leads both to wish to do whatever they see done without knowing very well what it is good for.

The great secret of education is to make the exercises of the body and of the mind always serve as a recreation for each other.

Émile [at fifteen] has little knowledge, but what he has is really his own; he knows nothing by halves.

He has a mind that is universal, not through its knowledge, but through its facility of acquiring it; a mind that is open, intelligent, ready for everything, and, as

Montaigne says, if not taught, at least teachable.   It is sufficient for me that he can find
the *What profits it* of everything he does,
and the *Why* of everything he believes.

From Fifteen to Twenty.

The study proper for man is that of his
relations.   While he knows himself only
through his physical being, he ought to
study himself through his relation with
things, and this is the occupation of his
childhood ; but when he begins to feel his
moral nature, he ought to study himself
through his relations with men, and this is
the occupation of his entire life, beginning at
the point we have now reached.

JOHANN FRIEDERICH HERBART.

"A psychologist of the first rank, the founder, some would call him, of modern psychology."—OSCAR BROWNING.

THE SCIENCE OF EDUCATION.[1]

Introduction.

THE whole power of what humanity has felt, experienced, and thought, is the true and right educator, to which the boy is entitled, and the teacher is given to him merely that he may help him by intelligent interpretation and elevating companionship. Thus to present the whole treasure of accumulated research in a concentrated form to the youthful generation, is the highest

---

[1] THE SCIENCE OF EDUCATION: *Its General Principles Deduced from its Aim, etc.*—By JOHANN FRIEDERICH HERBART. Translated from the German, with a Biographical Introduction by HENRY M. and EMMIE FELKIN, and a Preface by OSCAR BROWNING, M. A., King's College, Cambridge. American publishers, Boston, Mass.: D. C. HEATH & CO.

service which mankind at any period of its existence can render to its successors.

The first, though by no means the complete science of the educator, would be a psychology in which the total possibilities of human activity were sketched out *à priori*. I think I recognize the difficulty as well as the possibility of such a science. Long will it be before we have it, longer still before we can expect it from teachers. Never, however, can it be a substitute for observation of the pupil ; the individual can only be discovered, not deduced.

Character is inner stability, and how can a human being take root in himself, when he is not allowed to depend on anything, when , you do not permit him to trust a single decision to his own will ?

In most cases it happens, that the youthful soul has in its depths a sacred corner, into which you never penetrate, and in which, notwithstanding your rough treatment, it lives for itself, dreams, hopes, and evolves

plans which will be tried at the first opportunity, and if successful will base a character,
just on the very spot you did not know.
This is the reason why the aim and the result of education are wont to have so little
connection.

Those only wield the full power of education, who know how to cultivate in the
youthful soul a large circle of thought closely
connected in all its parts, possessing the
power of overcoming what is unfavorable
in the environment, and of dissolving and
absorbing into itself all that is favorable.

The Aim of Education.

Government which is satisfied without
education, oppresses the mind, and education which takes no heed of the disorderly
conduct of children, would not be recognized
as such by the children themselves.

The first measure that all government
has to take is the threat of punishment, and
in its use all government runs the danger of
striking on one of two rocks: on the one

side there are strong natures who despise all threats, and dare everything to gain their will ; on the other there are natures—a far greater number—who are too weak to be impressed by threats, and in whom fear itself is subservient to desire.

Suffice it briefly to remember that punctilious and constant supervision is burdensome alike to the supervisor and those he watches over, and is apt therefore to be associated on both sides with deceit, and thrown off at every opportunity—and also that the need for it grows with the degree in which it is used, and that at last every moment of its intermittence is fraught with danger.

I pass to the means of help which must be prepared in the children's minds themselves by government—I mean authority and love.

The mind bends to authority: . . . . But authority is only obtained through superiority of mind, and this, as is well known, cannot be reduced to rules. It must act independently, without reference to education.

Love depends on the harmony of the feelings and on habit. . . . The harmony of feelings love demands, may arise in two ways. Either the teacher enters into the feelings of the pupil, and without permitting it to be noticed, joins in them with tact, or he takes care that the feelings of the pupil can approach his own in some particular way.

Authority belongs most naturally to the father. . . . Love belongs most naturally to the mother. . . . If then authority and love are the best means of maintaining the effect of the child's earliest subjection, so far as its further government requires, it then of necessity follows, firstly, that this government will be best left in the hands of those to whom nature has intrusted it.

The fashioner of the mind, in whom at best only an ever limited trust is placed, should not in his pride desire to carry on his profession by himself alone, to the exclusion of the parents; he would thereby lose the power of their influence, for the loss of which he cannot easily find a compensation.

If, however, the government of children must devolve on persons other than the parents, it is important to carry it on with as little friction as possible. This depends on the proportion which the children's activity bears to the amount of free play they get. . . . When the environment is so arranged, that childish activity can itself find the track of the useful and spend itself thereon, then government is most successful.

Instant obedience following a command on the spot and with entire acquiescence, which teachers, not wholly without reason, look upon as their triumph—who would force this from children by merely cramping regulations as well as military severity ? Such obedience can only in reason be associated with the child's own will : this, however, is only to be expected as the result of a somewhat advanced stage of genuine education.

Education proper is cognizant, like government, of something which may be called compulsion ; it is indeed never harsh, but often very strict. . . . Education makes itself quite as oppressive, though less abruptly so, by constantly exacting that which is unwillingly done, and by obstinately ignoring the wishes of the pupil.

The sour-tempered person who is insensible to this feeling [sympathy with youth] would do better to avoid the young—he does not so much as understand how to look at them with proper consideration. Only he who receives much, and is therefore able to give much, can also deprive of much, and by such pressure mould the disposition and direct the attention of the youthful mind according to his own judgment.

Let there be no wearisome sulkiness, no artificial gravity, no mystical reserve, and, above all, no false friendliness. Honesty must be the soul of all activity, however numerous its changes of direction may be.

The pupil will have to test the teacher in

many ways, before there grows up that
subtle tractability which ought to spring
from mere knowledge of, and regard for his
feelings. When, however, it is manifested,
the teacher's attitude must be more steadfast, more equable ; he must not lay himself
open to the suspicion that no enduring
relationship is possible with him, or that his
heart is not a safe resting-place.

It is before all things necessary to observe
the manner in which moral culture is related
to the other parts of culture, that is to say,
how it (moral culture) presupposes them as
conditions from which alone it can with certainty be developed. Unprejudiced persons
will, I hope, easily see that the problem of
moral education is not separable from education as a whole, but that it stands in a
necessary, far-reaching connection with the
remaining problems of education.

The kingdom of the pupil's future aims at
once divides itself for us into the province
of *merely possible aims* which he might
perhaps take up at one time or other and

pursue in greater or less degree as he wishes —and into the entirely distinct province of the *necessary aims* which he would never pardon himself for having neglected. In one word, the aim of education is sub-divided according to the aims of *choice*—not of the teacher, nor of the boy, but of the future man, and the aims of *morality*.

(1) How can the teacher assume for himself beforehand the merely *possible* future aims of the pupil ? . . . . We call the first part of the educational aim —*many-sidedness of interest*, which must be distinguished from its exaggeration—dabbling in many things. And since no one object of will, nor its individual direction, interests us more than any other, we add to this, lest weakness may offend us by appearing by the side of strength, the predicate—*proportionate* many-sidedness.

(2) How is the teacher to assume for himself the *necessary* aims of the pupil ? . . . . That the ideas of the right and good in all their clearness and purity may become

the essential objects of the will, that the
innermost intrinsic contents of the character
—the very heart of the personality—shall
determine itself according to these ideas,
putting back all arbitrary impulses—this and
nothing less is the aim of moral culture.

The teacher aims at the universal ; the
pupil, however, is an individual human
being. . . . We know how beneficial it is
for mankind, that different men should
resolve upon and prepare for different work.
Moreover, the individuality of the youth
reveals itself more and more under the
teacher's efforts. . . . Out of all this there
results a negative rule in relation to the aim
of education, which is as important as it is
difficult to observe, *i. e.,* to leave the individuality untouched as far as possible.

Is *individuality* consistent with *many-
sidedness ?* . . . Our chief business is to distinguish most carefully between the different
chief concepts, *i. e.,* many-sidedness, interest, character, morality—for on them must

be directed all the labor which we propose to expend.

|Character] is WILL, and we mean will in the strict sense, which is far different from variations of temper or desire, for these are not *determined*, while the will on the contrary is.

The *kind* of the determination constitutes the character.   Willing—determination— takes place in consciousness.   Individuality, on the other hand, is unconscious.   It is the mysterious root to which our psychological heredity refers everything which, according to circumstances, comes out ever differently in human beings.

Character, then, almost inevitably expresses itself in opposition to individuality by conflict.

For it is simple and steadfast ; individuality, on the contrary, continually sends forth from its depths other and new thoughts and desires.

Many-sidedness has neither sex, nor rank, nor age.   With mental feelers everywhere, with ever-ready sensation, it suits men and girls, children and women ; .... Intolerance is in its eyes the only crime. .... Nothing is new to it ; but everything remains fresh.   Custom, prejudice, aversion, and torpor disturb it not.

Interest arises from interesting objects and occupations.   Many-sided interest originates in the *wealth* of these.   To create and develop this interest is the task of instruction, which carries on and completes the preparation begun by intercourse and experience.

Many-sidedness of Interest.

He who has at any time given himself up *con amore* to any object of human activity understands what concentration means. .... Personality rests on the unity of consciousness, on co-ordination, on Reflection. .... These processes cannot be contemporaneous ; they must therefore follow one upon the other ; we get first one act of concentration, then another, then their meeting in Reflection.

We must not do more here in the name of

many-sidedness than show generally the
necessity of reflection. To know beforehand
in what manner it is composed on every occasion of such concentrations would be the
business of psychology; to feel it by antici-
pation is the essence of educational tact, the
most precious treasure of the art of education.

Interest, which in common with desire,
will, and the esthetic judgment, stands opposed to indifference, is distinguished from
those three, in that it neither controls nor
disposes of its object, but depends upon it.
It is true that we are inwardly active because we are interested, but externally we
are passive till interest passes into desire or
volition.

The object of interest can never be iden-
tical with that which is in reality desired.
For the desires, while they would fain grasp,
strive towards some future object which they
do not already possess ; interest, on the other
hand, unfolds itself in observation, and clings
to the contemplated *present.* Interest only

rises above mere perception in that what it perceives possesses the mind by preference, and makes itself felt among the remaining perceptions by virtue of a certain causality.

It is inglorious to be absorbed by desires, and yet more inglorious to be absorbed by a multiplicity of desires. . . . Patient interest, on the contrary, can never become too rich, and the richest interest will be the most ready to remain patient. In it the character possesses a facility in accomplishing its resolves, which accompanies it everywhere, without frustrating its plans by pretentiousness.

To leave man to Nature, or even to wish to lead him to, and train him up in, Nature is merely folly. . . . We know our aim. Nature does much to aid us, and humanity has gathered much on the road she has already traversed ; it is our task to join them together.

From Nature man attains to knowledge through experience, and to sympathy through intercourse. . . . Experience and intercourse are often wearisome, and we must sometimes

bear it. But the pupil must never be con-
demned to suffer this from the teacher. To
be wearisome is the cardinal sin of instruction ; it is the privilege of instruction to fly
over steppes and morasses, and if it cannot
always wander in pleasant valleys, it can
train on the other hand in mountain climb-
ing and reward with the wider prospect.

Instruction must universally point out,
connect, teach, philosophize. In matters ap-
pertaining to sympathy it should be observing, continuous, elevating, active in the
sphere of reality.

Symbols are to instruction an obvious bur-
den which, if not lightened by the power of
interest in the thing symbolized, throws both
teacher and pupil out of the track of progressive culture. . . . Make therefore a stand
as long as possible against every instruction
in language without exception, which does
not directly lie on the high road of the culture of interest. Whether ancient or modern language it is all the same. That book
alone has a claim to be read which interests

now, and can prepare the way for fresh interest in the future.

Let every affected manner be banished from instruction ! . . . . The teacher must be capable of many happy turns, he must vary with facility, must adapt himself to opportunity, and while playing with the accidental must so much the more emphasize the essential.

All mannerisms that compel the listener's passivity, and extract from him a painful negation of his proper activity, are in themselves unpleasant and oppressive. . . . That manner is the best, which provides the greatest amount of freedom within the circle which the work in question makes necessary to preserve.

HERBERT SPENCER.

"The work which Herbert Spencer has done in organizing the different departments of human knowledge .... is work of the calibre of that which Aristotle and Newton did."—JOHN FISKE.

FROM "EDUCATION." [1]

What Knowledge Is of Most Worth?

HOW to live?—that is the essential question for us. Not how to live in the mere material sense only, but in the widest sense. .... how to use all our faculties to the greatest advantage of ourselves and others— how to live completely. And this being the great thing needful for us to learn, is, by consequence, the great thing which education has to teach.

The actions and precautions by which,

---

[1] EDUCATION : Intellectual, Moral, and Physical. By HERBERT SPENCER. New York : D. APPLETON & Co. (Copyright by D. APPLETON & Co., in 1860.)

from moment to moment, we secure personal safety, must clearly take precedence of
all others.

That next after direct self-preservation
comes the indirect self-preservation which
consists in acquiring the means of living,
none will question.

As the family comes before the State in
order of time—as the bringing up of children
is possible before the State exists, or when
it has ceased to be, whereas the State is
rendered possible only by the bringing up of
children ; it follows that the duties of the
parent demand closer attention than those of
the citizen.

Those various forms of pleasurable occupation which fill up the leisure left by graver
occupations—the   enjoyments   of   music,
poetry, painting, &c.—manifestly imply a
pre-existing society. . . . And, consequently,
that part of human conduct which constitutes good citizenship is of more moment
than that which goes out in accomplishments

or exercise of the tastes ; and, in education, preparation for the one must rank before preparation for the other.

After making all qualifications, there still remain these broadly-marked divisions ; and it still continues substantially true that these divisions subordinate one another in the foregoing order, because the corresponding divisions of life make one another *possible* in that order.

Happily, that all-important part of education which goes to secure direct self-preservation, is in great part already provided for. Too momentous to be left to our blundering, Nature takes it into her own hands. . . . What we are chiefly called upon to see, is that there shall be free scope for gaining this experience, and receiving this discipline, —that there shall be no such thwarting of Nature as that by which stupid school-mistresses commonly prevent the girls in their charge from the spontaneous physical activities they would indulge in ; and so render

them comparatively incapable of taking care
of themselves in circumstances of peril.

This, however, is by no means all that is
comprehended in the education that prepares
for direct self-preservation. Besides guard-
ing the body against mechanical damage or
destruction, it has to be guarded against injury from other causes—against the disease
and death that follow breaches of physiologic
law. . . . If any one doubts the importance
of an acquaintance with the fundamental
principles of physiology as a means to
complete living, let him look around and see
how many men and women he can find in
middle or later life who are thoroughly well.

In all cases [of physical disorder] a permanent damage is done—not immediately
appreciable, it may be, but still there ; and
along with other such items which Nature
in her strict account-keeping never drops,
will tell against us to the inevitable shorten-
ing of our days. Through the accumula-
tion of small injuries it is that the constitu-

tions are commonly undermined, and break down long before their time.

We infer that as vigorous health and its accompanying high spirits are larger elements of happiness than any other thing whatever, the teaching how to maintain them is a teaching that yields in moment to no other whatever. And therefore we assert that such a course of physiology as is needful for the comprehension of its general truths, and their bearings on daily conduct, is an all-essential part of a rational education.

We need not insist on the value of that knowledge which aids indirect self-preservation by facilitating the gaining of a livelihood.

Leaving out only some very small classes, what are all men employed in? They are employed in the production, preparation, and distribution of commodities. And on what does efficiency in the production, preparation, and distribution of commodities de-

pend? It depends on the use of methods
fitted to the respective natures of these commodities; it depends on an adequate knowledge of their physical, chemical, or vital
properties, as the case may be; that is, it
depends on science.

To all such as are occupied in the production, exchange, or distribution of commodities, acquaintance with science in some of
its departments, is of fundamental importance. Whoever is immediately or remotely
implicated in any form of industry (and few
are not) has a direct interest in understanding something of the mathematical, physical,
and chemical properties of things; perhaps,
also, has a direct interest in biology; and
certainly has in sociology.

What we call learning a business, really
implies learning the science involved in it;
though not perhaps under the name of science. And hence a grounding in science is
of great importance, both because it prepares
for all this, and because rational knowledge

has an immense superiority over empirical knowledge.

Is it not an astonishing fact, that though on the treatment of offspring depend their lives or deaths, and their moral welfare or ruin; yet not one word of instruction on the treatment of offspring is ever given to those who will hereafter be parents? Is it not monstrous that the fate of a new generation should be left to the chances of unreasoning custom, impulse, fancy—joined with the suggestions of ignorant nurses and the prejudiced counsel of grandmothers?

They [parents] have undertaken to control the lives of their offspring from hour to hour; with cruel carelessness they have neglected to learn anything about these vital processes which they are unceasingly affecting by their commands and prohibitions; in utter ignorance of the simplest physiologic laws, they have been year by year undermining the constitutions of their children; and have so inflicted disease and premature death, not only on them but on their descendants.

Equally great are the ignorance and the consequent injury, when we turn from physical training to moral training. . . . She [the young mother] knows nothing about the nature of the emotions, their order of evolution, their functions, or where use ends and abuse begins. She is under the impression that some of the feelings are wholly bad, which is not true of any one of them; and that others are good, however far they may be carried, which is also not true of any one of them. And then, ignorant as she is of that with which she has to deal, she is equally ignorant of the effects that will be produced on it by this or that treatment.

Lacking knowledge of mental phenomena, with their causes and consequences, her interference is frequently more mischievous than absolute passivity would have been. . . . While insisting on truthfulness she constantly sets an example of untruth, by threatening penalties which she does not inflict. While inculcating self-control, she hourly visits on her little ones angry scoldings for acts that do not call for them. She has not the remotest idea that in the nursery, as in the world, that alone is the truly salutary discipline which visits on all conduct, good and bad, the natural consequences—the consequences, pleasurable or painful, which in the nature of things such conduct tends to bring.

And then the culture of the intellect—is not this, too, mismanaged in a similar manner? Grant that the phenomena of intelligence conform to laws; grant that the evolution of intelligence in a child also conforms to laws; and it follows inevitably that education can be rightly guided only by a knowledge of these laws. To suppose that you can properly regulate this process of forming and accumulating ideas, without understanding the nature of the process, is absurd. How widely, then, must teaching as it is, differ from teaching as it should be; when hardly any parents, and but few teachers, know anything about psychology.

Some acquaintance with the first principles of physiology and the elementary truths of psychology is indispensable for the right bringing up of children.

From the parental functions let us pass now to the functions of the citizen. We have here to inquire what knowledge best fits a man for the discharge of these functions.

Were some one to tell you that your neighbor's cat kittened yesterday, you would say that the information was worthless. Fact though it might be, you would say that it was an utterly useless fact—a fact that could in no way influence your actions in life—a fact that would not help you in learning how to live completely. Well, apply the same test to the great mass of historical facts, and you will get the same result. They are facts from which no conclusions can be drawn—*unorganizable* facts; and therefore facts which can be of no service in establishing principles of conduct, which is the chief use of facts.

Only of late years have historians commenced giving us, in any considerable quantity, the truly valuable information. . . . Only now, when the welfare of nations rather than of rulers is becoming the dominant idea, are historians beginning to occupy themselves with the phenomena of social progress. That which it really concerns us to know, is the natural history of society. We want all facts which help us to understand how a nation has grown and organized itself.

Among these, let us of course have an account of its government : with as little as may be of gossip about the men who officered it, and as much as possible about the structure, principles, methods, prejudices, corruptions, &c., which it exhibited. . . . Let us of course also have a parallel description of the ecclesiastical government—its organization, its conduct, its power, its relations to the State. . . . Let us at the same time be informed of the control exercised by class over class, as displayed in all social

observances—in titles, salutations, and forms
of address.   Let us know, too, what were all
the other customs which regulated the popular life out of doors and in-doors : . . . Next
should come a delineation of the industrial
system : . . . Accompanying all which should
come an account of the industrial arts
technically considered : stating the processes
in use, and the quality of the products.
Further, the intellectual condition of the
nation in its various grades should be de-
picted : . . . The degree of esthetic culture
. . . . should be described.   Nor should
there be omitted a sketch of the daily lives
of the people—their food, their homes, and
their amusements.   And lastly, to connect
the whole, should be exhibited the morals,
theoretical and practical, of all classes : as
indicated in their laws, habits, proverbs,
deeds.

Such alone is the kind of information respecting past times, which can be of service
to the citizen for the regulation of his conduct.   The only history that is of practical

value, is what may be called Descriptive Sociology.

All social phenomena are phenomena of life—are the most complex manifestations of life—are ultimately dependent on the laws of life—and can be understood only when the laws of life [biology and psychology] are understood.

The current opinion that science and poetry are opposed, is a delusion. It is doubtless true that as states of consciousness, cognition and emotion tend to exclude each other. . . . But it is not true that the facts of science are unpoetical; or that the cultivation of science is necessarily unfriendly to the exercise of imagination or the love of the beautiful. On the contrary, science opens up realms of poetry where to the unscientific all is a blank.

Is it not, indeed, an absurd and almost a sacrilegious belief, that the more a man studies Nature the less he reveres it? . . . . The truth is, that those who have

never entered upon scientific pursuits know
not a tithe of the poetry by which they are
surrounded. Whoever has not in youth
collected plants and insects, knows not half
the halo of interest which lanes and hedge-
rows can assume. Whoever has not sought
for fossils, has little idea of the poetical
associations that surround the places where
imbedded treasures were found. Whoever
at the seaside has not had a microscope and
aquarium, has yet to learn what the highest
pleasures of the seaside are. Sad, indeed,
is it to see how men occupy themselves with
trivialities, and are indifferent to the grand-
est phenomena.

Thus far our question has been, the worth
of knowledge of this or that kind for purposes
of guidance. We have now to judge the
relative values of different kinds of knowledge for purposes of discipline. . . . It
would be utterly contrary to the beautiful
economy of Nature if one kind of culture
were needed for the gaining of information
and another kind were needed as a

mental gymnastic. . . . The education of most value for guidance, must at the same time be the education of most value for discipline.

While for the training of mere memory, science is as good as, if not better than, language; it has an immense superiority in the kind of memory it cultivates. In the acquirement of a language, the connections of ideas to be established in the mind correspond to facts that are in great measure accidental; whereas, in the acquirement of science, the connections of ideas to be established in the mind correspond to facts that are mostly necessary. . . . The relations which science presents are causal relations; and, when properly taught, are understood as such.

Correct judgment, with regard to all surrounding things, events, and consequences, becomes possible only through knowledge of the way in which surrounding phenomena depend on each other. . . . The constant habit of drawing conclusions from data, and then of verifying those conclusions by observation and experiment, can alone give the power of judgment correctly. And that it necessitates this habit is one of the immense advantages of science.

Not only, however, for intellectual discipline is science the best; but also for *moral* discipline. . . . By science, constant appeal is made to individual reason. Its truths are not accepted upon authority alone. . . . Every step in a scientific investigation is submitted to his judgment. He is not asked to admit it without seeing it to be true. Nor is this the only benefit bequeathed by scientific culture. When carried on, as it should always be, as much as possible under the form of independent research, it exercises perseverance and sincerity.

Lastly we have to assert . . . . that the discipline of science is superior to that of our ordinary education, because of the *religious* culture that it gives. . . . It generates a profound respect for, and an explicit faith in, those uniform laws which underlie all things. By accumulated experiences the man of science acquires a thorough belief in the unchanging relations of phenomena—in the invariable connection of cause and consequence—in the necessity of good or evil results. . . . He sees that the laws to which we must submit are not only inexorable but beneficent. He sees that in virtue of these laws, the process of things is ever towards a greater perfection and higher happiness. . . . And thus does he, by asserting the eternal principles of things and the necessity to conforming to them, prove himself intrinsically religious.

To all which add the further religious aspect of science, that it alone can give us true conceptions of ourselves and our relation to the mysteries of existence. At the same time that it shows us all which can be known, it shows us the limits beyond which we can know nothing. . . . Only the genuine man of science, we say, can truly know how utterly beyond, not only human knowledge, but human conception, is the Universal Power of which Nature, and Life, and Thought are manifestations.

Intellectual Education.

There can not fail to be a relationship between the successive systems of education, and the successive social states with which they have co-existed. Having a common origin in the national mind, the institutions of each epoch, whatever be their special functions, must have a family likeness. When men received their creed and its interpretations from an infallible authority deigning no explanations, it was natural that the teaching of children should be purely dogmatic.

The increase of political liberty, the abolition of law restricting individual action, and the amelioration of the criminal code, have been accompanied by a kindred progress towards non-coercive education : the pupil is hampered by fewer restraints, and other means than punishments are used to govern him.

Some centuries ago there was uniformity of belief—religious, political, and educational. . . . . The decline of authority, whether papal, philosophic, kingly, or tutorial, is essentially one phenomenon; in each of its aspects a leaning towards free action is seen alike in the working out of the change itself, and in the new forms of theory and practice to which the change has given birth.

Of the three phases through which human opinion passes—the unanimity of the igno-rant, the disagreement of the inquiring, and the unanimity of the wise—it is manifest that the second is the parent of the third. They are not sequences in time only; they are sequences in causation. However im-patiently, therefore, we may witness the present conflict of educational systems, and however much we may regret its accompany-ing evils, we must recognize it as a transition stage needful to be passed through, and beneficent in its ultimate effects.

The once universal practice of learning by rote, is daily falling more into discredit. . . . The rote-system, like other systems of its age, made more of the forms and symbols than of the things symbolized. To repeat the words correctly was everything; to understand their meaning, nothing; and thus the spirit was sacrificed to the letter.

Along with rote-teaching, is declining also the nearly allied teaching by rules. . . . While rules, lying isolated in the mind— not joined to its other contents as out-growths from them—are continually forgotten, the principles which those rules express piecemeal, become, when once reached by the understanding, enduring possessions. While the rule-taught youth is at sea when beyond the rules, the youth instructed in principles solves a new case as readily as an old one.

In following the process of nature, neither

individuals nor nations ever arrive at the science *first.* . . . In short, as grammar was made after language, so ought it to be taught after language; an inference which all who recognize the relationship between the evolution of the race and of the individual, will see to be unavoidable.

Of new practices that have grown up during the decline of the old ones, the most important is the systematic culture of the powers of observation. After long ages of blindness men are at last seeing that the spontaneous activity of the observing faculties in children has a meaning and a use. What was once thought [in children] mere purposeless action, or play, or mischief, as the case might be, is now recognized as the process of acquiring a knowledge on which all after-knowledge is based. Hence the well-conceived but ill-conducted system of *object-lessons.*

Indeed, if we consider it, we shall find that exhaustive observation is an element in all great success. It is not to artists, natural-

ists, and men of science only, that it is needful; it is not only that the skillful physician
depends on it for the correctness of his
diagnosis, and that to the good engineer it
is so important that some years in the work-
shop are prescribed for him; but we may
see that the philosopher also is fundamen-
tally one who *observes* relationships of things
which others had overlooked, and that the
poet, too, is one who *sees* the fine facts in
nature which all recognize when pointed out,
but did not before remark.

The truths of number, of form, of relationship in position, were all originally
drawn from objects; and to present these
truths to the child in the concrete is to let
him learn them as the race learnt them.

But of all the changes taking place, the
most significant is the growing desire to
make the acquirement of knowledge pleas-
ureable rather than painful—a desire based
on the more or less distinct perception that
at each age the intellectual action which a

child likes is a healthful one for it ; and con-
versely.

What now is the common characteristic
of these several changes? Is it not an in-
creasing conformity to the methods of
nature? . . . . For as it is the order of
nature in all creatures that the gratification
accompanying the fulfilment of needful
functions serves as a stimulus to their fulfilment—as during the self-education of the
young child, the delight taken in the biting
of corals, and the pulling to pieces of toys,
becomes the prompter to actions which
teach it the properties of matter ; it follows
that, in choosing the succession of subjects
and the modes of instruction which most
interest the pupil, we are fulfilling nature's
behests, and adjusting our proceedings to
the laws of life.

In education the process of self-develop-
ment should be encouraged to the fullest
extent. Children should be led to make
their own investigations, and to draw their
own inferences. They should be *told* as

littie as possible, and induced to *discover* as
much as possible.

As a final test by which to judge any
plan of culture, should come the question,—
Does it create a pleasurable excitement in
the pupils? When in doubt whether a
particular mode or arrangement is or is not
more in harmony with the foregoing principles than some other, we may safely abide
by this criterion. Even when, as considered
theoretically, the proposed course seems the
best, yet if it produce no interest, or less
interest than another course, we should re-
linquish it; for a child's intellectual instincts
are more trustworthy than our reasonings.

The earliest impressions that the mind can
assimilate, are those given to it by the un-
decomposable sensations—resistance, light,
sound, &c. . . . There can be no idea of
form until some familiarity with light in its
gradations and qualities, or resistance in its
different intensities, has been acquired; for,
as has been long known, we recognize visible form by means of varieties of light, and

tangible form by means of varieties of resistance. Similarly, no articulate sound is cognizable until the inarticulate sounds which go to make it up have been learned.

It needs but a glance at the daily life of the infant to see that all the knowledge of things which is gained before the acquirement of speech, is self-gained—that the qualities of hardness and weight associated with certain visual appearances, the possession of particular forms and colors by particular persons, the productions of special sounds by animals, the special aspects, are phenomena which it observes for itself.

And is not nature perpetually thrusting this method upon us, if we had but the wit to see it, and the humility to adopt it ? What can be more manifest than the desire of children for intellectual sympathy ? Mark how the infant sitting on your knee thrusts into your face the toy it holds, that you, too, may look at it. See when it makes a creak with its wet finger on the table, how it turns and looks at you ; does it again, and again looks

at you; thus saying as clearly as it can—
" Hear this new sound."

Is it not clear that we must conform our
course to these intellectual instincts—that we
must just systematize the natural process—
that we must listen to all the child has to tell
us about each object, must induce it to say
everything it can think of about such object,
must occasionally draw its attention to facts
it has not yet observed, with the view of
leading it to notice them itself whenever they
recur, and must go on by and by to indicate
or supply new series of things for a like exhaustive examination ?

To *tell* the child this and to *show* it the
other, is not to teach it how to observe, but
to make it a mere recipient of another's observations : a proceeding which weakens
rather than strengthens its powers of self-
instruction—which deprives it of the pleasures resulting from successful activity—
which presents this all-attractive knowledge
under the aspect of formal tuition—and which
thus generates that indifference and even

disgust with which these object-lessons are not unfrequently regarded.

Object-lessons should . . . . be extended to a range of things far wider, and continue to a period far later, than now. They should not be limited to the contents of the house ; but should include those of the fields and the hedges, the quarry and the sea-shore. They should not cease with early childhood ; but should be so kept up during youth as insensibly to merge into the investigations of the naturalist and the man of science.

If men are to be mere cits, mere porers over ledgers, with no ideas beyond their trades—if it is well that they should be as the cockney whose conception of rural pleasures extends no further than sitting in a tea-garden smoking pipes and drinking porter ; or as the squire who thinks of woods as places for shooting in, of uncultivated plants as nothing but weeds, and who classifies animals into game, vermin, and stock—then indeed it is needless for men to learn anything that does not directly help to replenish the till and fill the larder. But if there is a more worthy aim for us than to be drudges —if there are other uses in the things around us than their power to bring money —if there are higher faculties to be exercised than acquisitive and sensual ones—if the pleasures which poetry and art and science and philosophy can bring are of any moment—then is it desirable that the instinctive inclination which every child shows to observe natural beauties and investigate natural phenomena should be encouraged.

The spreading recognition of drawing as an element of education, is one amongst many signs of the more rational views on mental culture now beginning to prevail.

What is it that the child first tries to represent? Things that are large, things that are attractive in color, things round which its pleasurable associations most cluster— human beings from whom it has received so many emotions, cows and dogs which interest by the many phenomena they present, houses that are hourly visible and strike by their size and contrast of parts. And which of all the processes of representation gives it most delight ? Coloring. Paper and pencil are good in default of something better ; but a box of paints and a brush—these are the treasures.

Now, ridiculous as such a position will seem to drawing-masters, who postpone coloring and who teach form by a dreary discipline of copying lines, we believe that the course of culture thus indicated is the right one. That priority of color to form, which, as already pointed out, has a psychological basis, and in virtue of which psychological basis arises this strong preference in the child, should be recognized from the very beginning ; and from the very beginning also the things imitated should be real.

From all that has been said, it may be readily inferred that we wholly disapprove of the practice of drawing from copies ; and still more so of that formal discipline in making straight lines and curved lines and compound lines, with which it is the fashion of some teachers to begin.

Almost invariably, children show a strong propensity to cut out things in paper, to make, to build—a propensity which, if duly encouraged and directed, will not only prepare the way for scientific conceptions, but will develop those powers of manipulation in which most people are so deficient.

When the observing and inventive faculties have attained the requisite power, the pupil may be introduced to empirical geometry; that is—geometry dealing with methodical solutions, but not with the demonstrations of them. Like all other transitions in education, this should be made not formally but incidentally; and the relationship to constructive art should still be maintained.

The foregoing outlines of plans for exercising the perceptions in early childhood, for conducting object-lessons, for teaching drawing and geometry, must be considered as roughly-sketched illustrations of the method dictated by the general principles previously specified. We believe that on examination they will be found not only to progress from the simple to the complex, from the concrete to the abstract, from the empirical to the rational ; but to satisfy the further requirements that education shall be a repetition of civilization in little, that it shall be as much as possible a process of self-evolution, and that it shall be pleasurable.

Any piece of knowledge which the pupil has himself acquired, any problem which he has himself solved, becomes by virtue of the conquest much more thoroughly his than it could else be. The preliminary activity of mind which his success implies, the concentration of thought necessary to it, and the excitement consequent on his triumph, conspire to register all the facts in his memory in a way that no mere information heard from a teacher, or read in a school-book, can be registered.

Courage in attacking difficulties, patient concentration of the attention, perseverance through failures—these are characteristics which after-life specially requires; and these are characteristics which this system of making the mind work for its food specially produces.

As suggesting a final reason for making education a process of self-instruction, and consequence a process of pleasurable instruction, we may advert to the fact that, in proportion as it is made so, is there a probability that education will not cease when school days end. . . . When the acquisition of knowledge has been rendered habitually gratifying, then will there be as prevailing a tendency to continue, without superintendence, that same self-culture previously carried on under superintendence. These results are inevitable.

Moral Education.

The great error made by those who discuss questions of juvenile discipline, is in ascribing all the faults and difficulties to the

children, and none to the parents. The
current assumption respecting family government, as respecting national government,
is, that the virtues are with the rulers and
the vices with the ruled.

The truth is, that the difficulties of moral
education are necessarily of dual origin—
necessarily result from the combined faults
of parents and children.

When a child falls, or runs its head
against the table, it suffers a pain, the re-
membrance of which tends to make it more
careful for the future ; and by an occasional
repetition of like experiences, it is eventually
disciplined into a proper guidance of its
movements. . . . In these and like cases,
Nature illustrates to us in the simplest way,
the true theory and practice of moral discipline.

It is the peculiarity of these penalties, if
we must so call them, [of physical trans-
gression] that they are nothing more than
the *unavoidable consequences* of the deeds

which they follow : they are nothing more than the *inevitable reactions* entailed by the child's actions.

These painful reactions are proportionate to the degree in which the organic laws have been transgressed. A slight accident brings a slight pain, a more serious one, a greater pain.

These natural reactions which follow the child's wrong actions, are constant, direct, unhesitating, and not to be escaped. No threats : but a silent, rigorous performance. If a child runs a pin into its finger, pain follows. If it does it again, there is again the same result : and so on perpetually. In all its dealings with surrounding inorganic nature it finds this unswerving persistence, which listens to no excuse, and from which there is no appeal ; and very soon recognizing this stern though beneficent discipline, it becomes extremely careful not to transgress.

Still more significant will these general truths appear, when we remember that they

hold throughout adult life as well as
throughout infantine life. It is by an exper-
imentally-gained knowledge of the natural
consequences, that men and women are
checked when they go wrong.

Have we not here, then, the guiding principle of moral education ? . . . . Is it not
manifest that as "ministers and interpreters
of Nature" it is the function of parents to
see that their children habitually experience
the true consequences of their conduct—the
natural reactions : neither warding them off,
nor intensifying them, nor putting artificial
consequences in place of them ? No unprejudiced reader will hesitate in his assent.

The truly instructive and salutary consequences are not those inflicted by parents
when they take upon themselves to be
Nature's proxies ; but they are those inflicted by Nature herself.

In every family where there are young
children there almost daily occur cases of
what mothers and servants call " making a

litter." . . . . In most cases the trouble of rectifying this disorder falls anywhere but in the right place : . . . . In this very simple case, however, there are many parents wise enough to follow out, more or less consistently, the normal course—that of making the child itself collect the toys or shreds. The labor of putting things in order is the true consequence of having put them in disorder.

If the natural penalty be met by any refractory behavior (which it may perhaps be where the general system of moral discipline previously pursued has been bad), then the proper course is to let the child feel the ulterior reaction consequent on its disobedience. Having refused or neglected to pick up and put away the things it has scattered about, and having thereby entailed the trouble of doing this on some one else, the child should, on subsequent occasions, be denied the means of giving this trouble.

Right conceptions of cause and effect are early formed ; and by frequent and consis-

tent experience are eventually rendered definite and complete. Proper conduct in life
is much better guaranteed when the good
and evil consequences of action are ration-
ally understood, than when they are merely
believed on authority.

Another great advantage of this natural
system of discipline is, that it is a system of
pure justice ; and will be recognized by every
child as such. Whoso suffers nothing more
than the evil which obviously follows naturally from his own misbehavior, is much less
likely to think himself wrongly treated than
if he suffers an evil artificially inflicted on
him ; and this will be true of children as of
men.

How is this method to be applied to the
graver offences ? . . . . Note, in the first
place, that these graver offences are likely to
be both less frequent and less grave under
the *régime* we have described than under
the ordinary *régime*. . . . When, however,
such offences are committed, as they will
occasionally be even under the best system,

the discipline of consequences may still be resorted to ; and if there exist that bond of confidence and affection which we have described, this discipline will be found efficient. . . . . Where there exists a warm filial affection produced by a consistent parental friendship. . . . there the state of mind caused by parental displeasure will not only be salutary as a check to future misconduct of like kind, but will also be intrinsically salutary. The moral pain consequent upon having, for the time being, lost so loved a friend, will stand in place of the physical pain usually inflicted ; and where this attachment exists, will prove equally, if not more, efficient.

In brief, the truth is that savageness begets savageness, and gentleness begets gentleness. Children who are unsympathetically treated become relatively unsympathetic ; whereas treating them with due fellow-feeling is a means of cultivating their fellow-feeling.

Do not expect from a child any great

amount of moral goodness. During early years every civilized man passes through that phase of character exhibited by the barbarous race from which he is descended. . . . The popular idea that children are "innocent," while it may be true in so far as it refers to evil *knowledge*, is totally false in so far as it refers to evil *impulses*, as half an hour's observation in the nursery will prove to any one.

Not only is it unwise to set up a high standard for juvenile good conduct, but it is even unwise to use very urgent incitements to such good conduct. . . . Be content, therefore, with moderate measures and moderate results. Constantly bear in mind the fact that a higher morality, like a higher intelligence, must be reached by a slow growth; and you will then have more patience with those imperfections of nature which your child hourly displays.

Beware, however, of the two extremes ; not only in the respect of the intensity, but in respect of the duration of your displeasure. On the one hand, anxiously avoid that weak impulsiveness, so general among mothers, which scolds and forgives almost in the same breath. On the other hand, do not unduly continue to show estrangement of feeling, lest you accustom your child to do without your friendship, and so lose your influence over him.

Be sparing of commands. Command only in those cases in which other means are inapplicable, or have failed. . . . But whenever you *do* command, command with decision and consistency.

Bear constantly in mind the truth that the aim of your discipline should be to produce a *self-governing* being: not to produce a being to be *governed by others.*

You will have to carry on your higher education at the same time that you are educating your children. Intellectually you must cultivate to good purpose that most complex of subjects—human nature and its laws, as exhibited in your children, in yourself, and in the world. Morally, you must keep in constant exercise your higher feelings, and restrain your lower.

It will be seen that we have said nothing in this chapter about the transcendental distinction between right and wrong, of which wise men know so little, and children nothing. All thinkers are agreed that we may find the criterion of right in the effect of actions, if we do not find the rule there : and that is sufficient for the purpose we have had in view.

Physical Education.

On old and young, the pressure of modern life puts a still-increasing strain. In all businesses and professions, intenser competition taxes the energies and abilities of every adult ; and, with the view of better fitting the young to hold their place under this intenser competition, they are subject to a more severe discipline than heretofore.

That disastrous consequences must result

from this cumulative transgression might be predicted with certainty; and that they do result, every observant person knows. Go where you will, and before long there come under your notice cases of children, or youths, of either sex, more or less injured by undue study.

Nature is a strict accountant; and if you demand of her in one direction more than she is prepared to lay out, she balances the account by making a deduction elsewhere.

Let it never be forgotten that the amount of vital energy which the body at any moment possesses is limited; and that, being limited, it is impossible to get from it more than a fixed quantity of results.

In a child or youth the demands upon this vital energy are various and urgent. As before pointed out, the waste consequent on the day's bodily exercise has to be repaired; the wear of brain entailed by the day's study has to be made good; a certain additional growth of body has to be provided for; and also a certain additional growth of brain; add to which the amount of energy absorbed in the digestion of the large quantity of food required for meeting these many demands.

Hence, if in youth, the expenditure in mental labor exceeds that which nature has provided for; the expenditure for other purposes falls below what it should have been : and evils of one kind or other are inevitably entailed.

There is an antagonism between *growth* and *development*. By growth, as used in this antithetical sense, is to be understood *increase of size ;* by development, *increase of structure*. And the law is, that great activity in either of these processes involves retardation or arrest in the other.

This law is true not only of the organism as a whole, but of each separate part. The abnormally rapid advance of any part in respect of structure involves premature arrest of its growth ; and this happens with the organ of the mind as certainly as with any other organ.   The brain, which during early years is relatively large in mass but imperfect in structure, will, if required to perform its functions with undue activity, undergo a structural advance greater than is appropriate to the age ; but the ultimate effect will be a falling short of the size and power that would else have been attained.

But these results of over-education, disastrous as they are, are perhaps less disastrous than the results produced upon the health— the undermined constitution, the enfeebled energies, the morbid feelings.

Consider, then, how great must be the damage inflicted by undue mental excitement on children and youths. More or less of this constitutional disturbance will inevitably follow an exertion of brain beyond that which nature has provided for ; and when not so excessive as to produce absolute illness, is sure to entail a slowly accumulating degeneracy of *physique*.

It [the cramming system] is a terrible mistake, from whatever point of view regarded. It is a mistake in so far as the mere acquirement of knowledge is concerned ; for it is notorious that the mind, like the body, cannot assimilate beyond a certain rate. . . . It is a mistake, too, because it tends to make study distasteful. . . . It is a mistake, also, inasmuch as it assumes that the acquisition of knowledge is everything ; and forgets that a much more important matter is the organization of knowledge, for which time and spontaneous thinking are requisite. . . . It is not the knowledge stored up as intellectual fat which is of value ; but that which is turned into intellectual muscle.

But the mistake is still deeper. Even were the system good as a system of intellectual training, which it is not, it would still be bad, because, as we have shown, it is fatal to that vigor of *physique* which is needful to make intellectual training available in the struggle of life.

Perhaps nothing will so much hasten the time when body and mind will both be ade-

quately cared for, as a diffusion of the belief
that the preservation of health is a *duty*.
Few seem conscious that there is such a
thing as physical morality.

The fact is, that all breaches of the laws of
health are *physical sins*.   When this is generally seen, then, and perhaps not till then,
will the physical training of the young receive
all the attention it deserves.

WILLIAM T. HARRIS.

FROM " PSYCHOLOGIC FOUNDATIONS OF EDUCATION." [1]

Introduction.

SOME knowledge of the mind every successful teacher must have, although in so many cases it is unsystematic, and consequently unscientific. . . . Science compensates the inequability of individual experience by reinforcing it with the aggregate of all other experiences.

In rational psychology we learn that there are three stages of the development of the thinking power. The first stage is that of sense-perception; its form of thinking conceives all objects as having independent being and as existing apart from all relation to other objects. . . .

[1] A volume in THE INTERNATIONAL EDUCATION SERIES This volume is written, and the series is edited, by WM. T. HARRIS, A.M., LL. D. *United States Commissioner of Education.* New York : D. APPLETON & CO., 1898.

The second stage of knowing is that which sees everything as depending upon the environment. Everything is relative, and can not exist apart from its relation to other things. . . .

The third stage of thinking arrives at the insight that true being is self-active or self-determined. True being is therefore self-conscious being, and exists as intellect and will ; all else is phenomenal being—On this insight depend the doctrines of God, freedom, and immutability. . . .

The most important end of intellectual education is to take the pupil safely through the world theory of the first and second stages—namely, sense-perception and the relativity doctrine—up to the insight into the personal nature of the absolute. All parts and pieces of school education should have in mind this development of the intellect.

The most important discovery ever made in psychology is this one of the three ascending steps or grades of thought which any one may take with due study and meditation. It is attributed to Plato.

The Psychology of Infancy.

For the first four years of the child's life the family education has been all in all for him. . . .

Imitation precedes the acquisition of language. In his third and fourth years the child's knowledge of the external world has progressed steadily, powerfuly aided, as it is now, by the acquisition of language ; for by language the child has become able to use the senses of other people as well as his own.

The place of imitation in the development of civilized man is beginning to be recognized. . . . The study of imitation leads to the discovery of the modes by which the individual man repeats for himself the thinking and doing and feeling of his fellows, and thus enriches his own life by adding to it the lives of others.

To see the significance of imitation in the child-mind, we must look upon it not as comparatively feeble and mechanical effort, as something determined by outside influences, but as a phase of self-activity which is engaged in emancipating the self from heredity and natural impulse.

There is an element of originality in the most mechanical phase of imitation. The self is active and assimilative. It sees an external deed which it proceeds to make its own deed by imitation.

In the acquirement of language the child has come into possession of the most powerful instrument of self-education that exists, and he has acquired a new faculty of mind—the faculty of seeing each object before the senses in the light of its universal—that is to say, he sees the real with a margin of ideal possibilities all around it. Ever after he will see any example or specimen that comes under a class name with a reflection that the previous specimen differed from it in some respects of size or color or shape. He will think of the other possibilities not realized whenever he sees any given real specimen of a class. Here, therefore, begins the child's perception of ideals.

The period of infancy is dominated by what may be called the symbolic stage of mind. . . .

There must be distinguished the following stages of symbolism :

(*a*) Personification : the placing of a soul in a thing : animism.

(*b*) Metaphor : the elevation of thing to a spiritual meaning (thing to soul, as personification makes soul to thing.)

(*c*) Play : one thing substituted for another : " Make believe that this stick is a horse ; " " I have built a house with these blocks ; " " This is the way the farmer mows his grass."

(*d*) The unconscious symbolic in poetry and mythology. It uses typical characters, shrouding the human in the forms of animals in fairy stories and fables.

The step from the image of a material object by symbolism to a spiritual relation shows a progress. . . . But the more familiar this step becomes the less time is occupied in imaging the material object, and the accent is placed more sharply on the thought of the spiritual object. By and by the image of the material object drops away almost entirely, and the word becomes a conventional sign for the spiritual thought and the mind forgets the sensuous meaning. This is the passage from the symbolic to the conventional stage of the mind, and takes place at a well-defined epoch in the life of the child in modern civilization. In savage life it is never reached. The mind remains at the myth-making or symbolic stage.

When the child possesses language and begins to inquire for names, begins to see ideals and to act to realize them, he can be helped greatly by the kindergarten method of instruction. . . . The kindergarten wisely selects a series of objects that lead to the useful possession of certain geometric concepts and numerical concepts that assist in grasping all things in their inorganic aspects. . . . . The kindergarten, in using the gifts and occupations, however, does not use the highest and best that Froebel has invented. The peculiar Froebel device is found in the plays and games.

The kindergarten does well when it teaches the gifts and occupations, for it deals with the world of means and instrumentalities, and helps the child to the conquest of Nature. It does better with the plays and games, because these are thoroughly humane in their nature, and they offer to the child in a symbolic form a first version of the experience of the race in solving the problem of life.

After the symbolic comes what is called the conventional. . . . The child, in fact, has arrived at a point where he needs instruments of self-help ; he needs to master the conventionalities of human learning ; he needs to learn how to read and write, and how to record the results of arithmetic. . . . This must be done by individual industry, and is an ethical deed quite distinct from the work of the child in the kindergarten. The child now feels the impulse of duty,

Self-subordination to reasonable tasks is no
longer play. He has arrived at the transition from play to work.

Psychology of the Course of Study in Schools.

There are five windows of the soul,
which open out upon five great divisions of
the life of man. . . .

The studies of the school fall naturally
into these five co-ordinate groups; first,
mathematics and physics; second, biology,
including chiefly the plant and the animal;
third, literature and art, including chiefly the
study of literary works of art; fourth, grammar and the technical and scientific study of
language, leading to such branches as logic
and psychology; fifth, history and the study
of sociological, political, and social institutions. Each one of these groups should be
represented in the curriculum of the schools
at all times by some topic suited to the age
and previous training of the pupil.

The elementary course of study is adapted

to the first eight years of school life, say from the age of six to that of fourteen years. That course of study deals chiefly with giving the child a mastery over the symbols of reading, writing, and arithmetic, and the technical words in which are expressed the distinctions of arithmetic, geography, grammar, and history. The child has not yet acquired much knowledge of human nature, nor of the world of things and forces about him. He has a tolerably quick grasp of isolated things and events, but he has very small power of synthesis. He cannot combine in his little mind things and events so as to perceive whole processes. It is the business of the school to induct him by easy steps into these things.

It is a necessary characteristic of primary or elementary instruction that it must take the world of human learnings in fragments, and fail to give its pupil an insight into the interrelation of things. It is the constant effort of good teaching to correct this defect.

There is a great difference between the teacher who requires only isolated details of his pupils and the one who directs their attention toward the relations and interdependences from the beginning. The true teaching aims always to strengthen the power of seizing relations. It cultivates the power of thought.

The education of high schools, academies, and preparatory schools—what we call secondary schools—begins to correct this inadequacy of elementary education. It begins to see things and events as parts of processes, and to understand their significance by tracing them back to their causes and forward to their results. . . . Where the pupil in the elementary school studies arithmetic and solves problems in particular numbers, the secondary pupil studies algebra and solves problems in general terms. Each algebraic formula is a rule for the performance of an indefinite number of arithmetical examples. In geometry, the secondary pupil learns necessary relations of spatial forms. In general history, he studies the collisions of one nation with another, and learns to interpret all the events in the light of the principle involved in the struggle. In science, he learns the forms and relations of Nature's phenomena. In the study of foreign languages he notes the variation of words to indicate relations of syntax; he investigates the structure of language, in which is revealed the degree of consciousness of the people who made that language.

But secondary education does not connect in any adequate manner the intellect and the will. It does not convert intellectual perceptions into rules of action. This is left for higher education.

The youth of proper age to enter on higher education has already experienced much of human life, and has arrived at the point where he begins to feel the necessity for a regulative principle, or a principle that shall guide him in deciding the endless questions which press upon him for settlement. Taking the youth at this epoch, when he begins to inquire for a principle, the college gives him a compend of human experience.

The person who has had merely an elementary schooling has laid stress on the mechanical means of culture—on the arts of reading, writing, computing, and the like. He has trained his mind for the acquirement of isolated details. . . . He has not yet learned the difference between knowledge and wisdom, or, what is better, the method of converting knowledge into wisdom.

It is evident that the individual who has received only an elementary education is at great disadvantage as compared with the person who has received a higher education in the college or university, making all allowances for the imperfections of existing institutions.

Very few persons change their methods after they leave school. Hence the importance of reaching the influence of the method of higher education before one closes his school career.

All the influences of the university, its distinguished professors, its venerable reputation, the organization of the students and professors as an institutional whole, combined with the isolation of the student from the strong ties of the home and the home community—all these taken together are able to effect this change in method when brought to bear upon a youth for four years. He acquires an attitude of mind which may be best described as critical and comparative.

FROM " HOW FAR MAY THE STATE PROVIDE EDUCATION AT PUBLIC COST ? "

In all countries the military education is at public expense. Where does the support and education of the nobility and royal families come from, except from the public? . . . . But in our country, where each is born to all the rights of mankind without distinction, all must be provided for.

It is, indeed, a great thing to have one class of society educated. No doubt, all profit by it, even when the education is con-

fined to a few.   But in a democracy all must
be educated, the interest of property demands
it, the interest of the government demands it.

The statistics of penitentiaries show that
a very small per cent. of well-educated men
are incarcerated.   The public schools send
very few. . . .   Self-directed   intelligence
makes for itself avenues for employment.
Nothing is lost.   Directive power finds it
easier to secure a competence by industry
than by intrigue and rascality.

The discipline of our Public Schools
wherein punctuality and regularity are enforced and the pupils are continually taught
to *suppress mere self-will* and inclination,
is the best school for morality.

ADDRESS ON HORACE MANN.

In studying the records of Massachusetts,
one is impressed by the fact that every new
movement in education has run the gauntlet
of fierce and bitter opposition before adoption.   The ability of the conservative party
has always been conspicuous, and the friends

of the new measure have been forced to exert all their strength, and to eliminate one after another the objectionable features discovered in advance by their enemies. To this fact is due the success of so many of the reforms and improvements that have proceeded from this State.

We are apt to become impatient and blame too severely the conservative party in Massachusetts.

We forget that the opposition helped to perfect the theory of the reform, and did much to make it a real advance instead of a mere change from one imperfect method to another. Even at best, educational changes are often only changes of fashion—the swing of the pendulum from one extreme to another—and sure to need correction by a fresh reaction.

Take as an instance of this the use of text-books. Every one will admit that what is called the " slavish use " of such means is a great evil. The memorizing of words and sentences, without criticism and reflection on their meaning, is a mechanical training of the mind and fit only for parrots. But, on the other hand, the proper use of the printed page is the greatest of all arts taught in the school. . . . For real progress comes from availing one's self of the wisdom of the race and using it as an instrument of new discovery.

That other method sometimes commended, of original investigation without aid from books, forgets that mankind has toiled for long thousands of years to construct a ladder of achievement and that civilization is on the highest round of this ladder. It has invented school education in order that its youth may climb quickly to the top on the rounds which have been added one by one, slowly, in the lapse of ages.

FROM "THE PHILOSOPHY OF EDUCATION."

Problems Peculiar to American Education.[1]

There are two kinds of education. The

---

[1] Johns Hopkins University Studies in Historical and Political Science. 1893.

first may be called Substantial Education—the education by means of the memory; the education which gives to the individual, methods and habits and the fundamentals of knowledge. . . . This is education by authority.

The second kind may be called individual or scientific education ; it is the education of insight as opposed to that of authority.

There is this danger in the system of education by insight, if begun too early, that the individual tends to become so self-conceited with what he considers knowledge gotten by his own personal thought and research, that he drifts towards empty agnosticism with the casting overboard of all authority. It is, therefore, necessary that this excessive conceit of self which this modern scientific method of education fosters, be lessened by building on the safe foundations of what has been described as the education of authority.

There is another problem—that of the

knowledge : we explain it in terms of the old ; we classify it ; identify it ; reconcile what is strange and unfamiliar in it with previous experience : we interpret the object and comprehend it ; we translate the unknown into the known.

This process of adjusting, explaining, classifying, identifying, reconciling, interpreting and translating is called *apperception.* We must not only perceive, but we must apperceive ; not only see and hear, but digest and assimilate what we hear and see.

Herbart's " apperception " is far more important for education than Pestalozzi's " perception ". . . . The course of study in schools must be arranged so as to prepare the mind for quick apperception of what is studied.

Herbert Spencer, and " What Knowledge Is of Most Worth."

Spencer calls education the subject which involves all other subjects, and the one in which they should all culminate. But some one has better said that school education is the giving to man the possession of the instrumentalities of intelligence. By his school education he does not attain all education, but he gets the tools of thought by which to master the wisdom of the race.

The first or elementary education is but superficial, a mere inventory : the secondary insists on some reflection on what has been learned; and the third, or higher education, is the unity and comparison of all that has been learned, so that each is explained by the whole. Give the child the embryology of civilization, and his insight into the evolution of civilization is insured.

FROM " REPORT: COMMISSIONER OF EDUCATION."—1897.

While the education of the American people supported by taxes and public funds is becoming more and more rigidly secular in character and the lines drawn more closely which separate it from ecclesiastical and religious instruction, yet the true importance of religious instruction is coming to be better understood among scientific and philosophical thinkers.

The secular institutions of man are organized as the family, civil society and the state. These provide for education, the procurement of the necessities of life, and the establishment of justice. But all of these presuppose a deeper ground in the ideal of the origin and destiny of man and nature. They involve a world view, and religion furnishes and must furnish a world view. Hence all people, whether connected with one or another denomination of Christians, or whether holding a religion other than Christian or holding no conscious religion at all, must admit the importance of the religious instruction of the community.

The secular school gives positive instruction. It teaches mathematics, natural science, history and language. Knowledge of the facts can be precise and accurate, and a similar knowledge of the principles can be arrived at. The self-activity of the pupil is before all things demanded by the teacher of the secular school. The pupil must not take things on authority, but must test and verify what he has been told by his own activity.

On the other hand religion, which gives the net result of the wisdom of the race in the form of authority, omits and must omit the long lines of proof which have established it.

Religious education, it is obvious, in giving the highest results of thought and life to the young, must cling to the form of authority, and not attempt to borrow the methods of mathematics, science, and history from the secular school. Such borrowing will result only in giving the young people an overweening confidence in the finality of their own immature judgments. They will become conceited and shallow-minded.

Against this danger of sapping or undermining all authority in religion by the introduction of the methods of the secular school which lay all stress on the self-activity of the child, the Sunday school has not been sufficiently protected in the more recent years of its history. Large numbers of religious teachers, most intelligent and zealous in their piety, seek a more and more perfect adoption of the secular school methods. . . . That method is not adapted to teach mystic truth. It seeks everywhere definite and especially mathematical results. But these results, although they are found everywhere in science and mathematics, are the farthest possible from being like the subject-matter of religon.

At present more and more attention is being given in the schools of civilized peoples to the training of pupils in esthetic taste. Those nations, other things being equal, are the richest that give their goods a beautiful finish and that introduce tasteful ornamentation. This accounts largely for the first rank held by France and Great Britain in the markets of the world.

The next step after the development of

the personal work of art in the shape of beautiful youth, by means of the national games and the cultivation of the taste of the entire people through the spectacle of these games, was the art of sculpture, by which these forms of beauty, realized in the athletes and existing in the minds of the people as ideals of correct taste, were fixed in stone and set up in the temples for worship. Thus Greek art was born.

It is not their resemblance to living bodies, not their anatomical exactness, that interests us, not their so-called "truth to nature," but their gracefulness and serenity—their "classic repose." . . . . In the greatest activity there is considerate purpose and perfect self-control manifested. The repose is of the soul, and not a physical repose. . . . The bearing of exhibits of Greek art on American industrial education is obvious.

One will concede at the start that tool work is valuable as industrial training, and that especially is this the case with the course of study and work in the manual-training school. . . . Still more valuable must we regard the study of natural science, and especially of applied mathematics, in the laws of matter and motion. . . . Besides this, we may claim that general education is of the utmost importance, opening as it does the powers of thought and observation, giving each laborer an insight into human nature and fitting him for logical thinking on all subjects; fitting him alike to lead others and combine them in extensive undertakings, and likewise to serve faithfully and intelligently other leaders when the case requires. . . . But esthetic education—the cultivation of taste, the acquirement of knowledge on the subject of the origin of the idea of beauty (both its historic origin and the philosophical account of its source in human nature), the practice of producing the outlines of the beautiful by the arts of drawing, painting, and modeling, the criticism of works of art with a view to discover readily the causes of failure or of success in esthetic effects—all these things, we must claim, form the true foundation of the highest success in the industries of any modern nation.

The dynamic side is needed ; but invention of the useful does not succeed in controlling the markets of the world. A nation with its laborers all educated in their taste for beautiful forms will give graceful shapes to their productions, and command higher prices for them.

In 1851, at the World's Exposition in London, it became evident that English industries were not of such a character as to compete with those of France and Belgium. Prince Albert, always wise and thoughtful, set about a deep-reaching system of education that should correct the national defect and recover the prestige of British arts and manufactures. . . . There began from this time a gradual rise in the taste of the English workman ; from being an artisan pure and simple he began to be an artist. England has gone forward rapidly in the direction of producing works of taste, and her useful manufactures, heretofore made without much reference to beauty, have steadily improved-in tastefulness of design and execution.

The establishment of a great national art gallery, the Louvre, and the studies of French savants in the canons of good taste, had long before revolutionized French manufactures, and given France the supremacy in the world-market for goods that command high prices and ready sale.

Taking hint from England, we have had in this country something of a fever for education in art, especially in the lines of industrial drawing. Remarkable as has been our progress in this matter, yet there is a prevalent lack of insight into the true direction and significance of this branch.

FROM " THE IMITATIVE FUNCTIONS IN CHILDHOOD." [1]

Imitation, in its purest and simplest form, that of mechanical repetition of the actions

---

[1] Paper read before the National Council of Education at Asbury Park, N. J., July 7, 1894.

of another person is, by common consent, placed at the bottom of spiritual achievements. A monkey or a parrot can mimic actions or speech, and to call the action of a human being parrot-like repetition, or a process of aping, is to express reproach and contempt for it.

But there is a consideration connected with imitative action which makes it the most fruitful approach to psychology, for it explains the mode in which the individual man unites with his fellow-men to form a social whole. It introduces us to the formation of institutions, the family, civil community, the State, the church—those greater selves which reinforce the little selves of isolated individuals. For the study of imitation leads to the discovery of the modes by which the individual man repeats for himself the thinking and doing and feeling of his fellows, and thus enriches his own life by adding to it the lives of others. Thus his own life becomes vicarious for others, and he participates vicariously in the life of society.

Imitation develops, on the one hand, into habits, or customs and morals, and this is the will-side of human mind ; and, on the other hand, it develops into perception, memory, ideas, and insights, this being the intellectual side of mind. It is evident that the pedagogic interest in psychology is the evolution of the higher faculties out of the lower.

It is necessary, first of all, to discover the most elementary forms of imitation. In this research the students of physical phenomena have greatly aided. The discovery of the fact that a small per cent. of people are so sensitive to the mental influences about them that they can, without the intermediation of words, read the thoughts of others has been made and verified in numerous instances. . . . The phrase " hypnotic suggestion " has come to play a great rôle in elucidating the rudimentary facts in imitation. . . . The rapid progress of scientific investigation in this field of psychic research promises to throw light on all social thought, feeling, and action. It will help us to understand much that has been obscure in the rise and spread of popular beliefs, the genesis of social tornadoes, like the Crusades, the French Revolution, the Tartaric invasions of Europe, or even such social affairs as strikes and mobs.

We must not lose sight of the essential fact that shows itself even in the most rudimentary of the phenomena of imitation. There can be no imitation whatever except on the part of self-active beings ; in other words, only souls can imitate.

The pride and pleasure that the infant exhibits on the occasion of his first conscious imitation has its root in this, that he has made something his own, has proved himself equal to imitating a movement in himself by his will ; he has revealed his selfhood to some extent. This is the significance of play, which is chiefly imitation, that the undeveloped human being is learning to know himself by seeing what he can do. He is revealing himself to others and to himself, and getting strength in his individuality.

Thus we see that there is an element of originality in the most mechanical phase of imitation. The self is active and assimilative. It sees an external deed, which it proceeds to make its own deed by imitation. . . . . Originality grows by progressive deepening of the insight into causes and motives of the things imitated. . . . There comes a time when the imitative child comprehends the principle as well as does the master whom he imitates, and then he is emancipated from all imitation in this part of his education. If he keeps on and comprehends the genesis of the principle from deeper principles, he emancipates himself from even the " hypnotic suggestion " of the principle itself, and all external authority has become inward freedom.

Here, in the stages of orginality, where the person has learned to comprehend what he once imitated, and now understands it in its causes and in the reasons for its existence, is self-imitation, if we are to speak of imitation at all. It is no longer an activity at an outward suggestion, but purely spontaneous. It has vanquished the external object by ascending to its causes.

FROM "A BRIEF FOR LATIN."[1]

The Latin language is by common consent an essential part of higher education as conducted in the colleges, universities, professional and technical schools of the United States. . . . In fact the number studying Latin [in the preparatory schools] is much larger than the number fitting for college or higher institutions, showing a conviction in the minds of the people that Latin is not merely an ornamental study but a useful study.

But the revival of the study of Latin has extended also to the elementary course of instruction which includes the first eight years of school work, or, loosely stated, the pupils from six to fourteen years of age.

---

[1] Educational Review. New York : April, 1899.

An active movement has begun in later years to give a portion of these first eight years to the study of Latin, and a large number of schools now commence Latin in the eighth year of the course and some of them begin the study of Latin either in the eighth or the seventh year.

To the countries using the romance languages,—France, Spain, Portugal, and Italy, —this revival of the study of Latin may seem strange, but it is easily explained when one considers the composition of the English language which, though Germanic or Teutonic in its colloquial vocabulary and in its grammatical structure, nevertheless resorts to the Latin and Greek for all its technical words and for all those words which express fine distinctions of thought or subtile shades of sentiment.

Any large dictionary of English includes in its vocabulary three words of Latin or Greek origin out of every four. While good English contains comparatively few of these Latin and Greek terms on a printed page,—

rarely more than from 10 to 16 per cent.,—yet it will be found that whatever is precise and technical in expression, as well as whatever contains fine discriminations of thought or delicate shades of feeling, is expressed in words of Latin origin.

In order to understand and use with propriety a technical term or a word expressing fine discrimination it is necessary to understand the colloquial word which corresponds to it; this is generally a word denoting things or events perceivable by the senses.

The illiterate German understands the word *Wissenschaft* because he recognizes the word *wissen* in it which he uses every day to express the act of knowing; but the Englishman uses the word *science* and cannot recognize in it the root *sci*, which means to know, unless he is acquainted with Latin.

A little study of Latin, such as is given in the high schools and academies, is therefore very useful to the English thinker, because it enables him to use with certainty and precision the words which express the results of careful thinking.

In a broader sense, however, Latin is essential to secondary and higher education for all European peoples, in fact for all the peoples which have derived their civilization from the Romans. It is found that in all the modern languages of Europe the distinctions of thought regarding the acquirement and transfer of property, and the formation of individuals into corporations for municipal or for business purposes, are of Latin derivation.

For the most part, the words expressing civil and political relations in all the languages of Europe are Latin.

In view of these considerations it is obvious that schools for secondary and for elementary, as well as for higher, instruction suffer injury if a rule excluding Latin from the course of study is rigidly enforced.

NICHOLAS MURRAY BUTLER.

FROM " THE MEANING OF EDUCATION." [1]

Introduction.

EDUCATION, in the broad sense in which I use the term, is the most important of human interests, since it deals with the preservation of the culture and efficiency that we have inherited, and with their extension and development ; . . . . This human interest can and should be studied in a scientific spirit and by a scientific method ; . . . . In a democracy at least an education is a failure that does not relate itself to the duties and opportunities of citizenship.

To give to education its rightful place in

---

[1] THE MEANING OF EDUCATION, and OTHER ESSAYS AND ADDRESSES. By NICHOLAS MURRAY BUTLER, Professor of Philosophy and Education in Columbia University. New York: MACMILLAN COMPANY, 1898.

our thinking involves relating it to the laws of life in general, and especially to those laws as viewed from the standpoint of the doctrine of evolution. . . . In this way the theory of education is given what it has hitherto lacked, a distinct relationship to the facts of organic and social evolution.

A standard must next be sought by which the value of educational processes and influences may be judged. I find this standard in the conclusion, common, I am confident, to the best philosophy and to the soundest science alike, that the facts of nature must be explained, in the last resort, in terms of energy, and that energy in turn can be conceived only in terms of will, which is the fundamental form of the life of mind or spirit.

I offer these two conclusions as the basis for an educational philosophy.

The Meaning of Education.

The child receives first, and in a short series of years, his animal inheritance; it

then remains for us in the period of education to see to it that he comes into his human
inheritance.

The great educational temple of modern
times into which every civilized nation is
pouring out its strength and its treasure,
rests upon the two corner-stones of the
physical and psychical nature of the child
and the traditional and hereditary civilization of the race. . . . The problem of the
family, of the school, and of the home, is to
unite those two elements so that each shall
possess the other. We shall then have a
conception of education which is in accord
with the doctrine of evolution, and which is
in accord with the teachings of modern
science and of modern philosophy.

The scientific inheritance is one of the
very first elements of a modern liberal education, because it is that element which presents itself earliest to the senses of the child.
It is the element with which he comes in
immediate sense-contact ; to which he can
be first led ; from which he may be made to

understand and draw lessons of the deepest significance for his life and for that adaptation which is his education.

Just as scientific method is the gate to the scientific inheritance and therefore must in essence at least be mastered, so language is the gate to the literary inheritance and must be mastered at the earliest opportunity. . . . Language is the crystallized thought of the past. It contains in itself, in its products and its forms, in its delicate discriminations, its powers of comparison and abstraction, a record of the progress of the thought of the race.

In the education that is sometimes called " new," it will be found that the earliest linguistic exercises are almost always based upon something that is really worth knowing for its own sake. Our literatures the world over, ancient and modern, are so rich, so full of thought and feeling and action, that there is no time to waste in the merely formal exercises of grammatical drill upon lifeless material, when we may be occupying ourselves, in those same exercises and for the same purpose of discipline, with material that enriches the human mind and touches and refines the human heart.

The third element in education is the esthetic inheritance, that feeling for the beautiful, the picturesque, and the sublime, that has always been so great a part of human life, that contributes so much to human pleasure and accentuates so much of human pain and suffering.

To-day we find art creeping into the school-room; instruction in color, in form, in expression is being given. The growing child is surrounded with representations of the classic in art, and so, unconsciously and by imitation, he is being taught to adapt and adjust himself to this once forgotten and now recovered element in human civilization; an element that certainly is, like the scientific and literary elements, an integral part of the child's inheritance.

Then there is also the wonderful institutional inheritance, most wonderful of all, because it brings us into immediate contact with the human race itself.

We have wrested that institutional life from history, and it is going to-day into the education of children all over the civilized world. In this way they are being given their institutional inheritance ; they are being given some insight not alone into their rights, which are so easy to teach, but into their duties, which are so easy to forget ; and the institutional life that carries with it lessons of duty, responsibility and the necessity for co-operation in the working out of high ideals, is being put before children wherever sound education is given to-day, from the kindergarten to the university.

Finally, there is the religious inheritance of the child. No student of history can doubt its existence and no observer of human nature will undervalue its significance. We are still far from comprehending fully the preponderant influence of religion in shaping our contemporary civilization; an influence that is due in part to the universality of religion itself, and in part to the fact that it was, beyond dispute, the chief human interest at the time when the foundations of our present superstructure were being laid.

The growing tendency toward what is known as the separation of church and state, but what is more accurately described as the independence of man's political and religious relationships, and, concurrently, the development of a public educational conscience which has led the state to take upon itself a large share of the responsibility for education, have brought about the practical exclusion of the religious element from public education.

Yet the religious element may not be permitted to pass wholly out of education unless we are to cripple it and render it hopelessly incomplete. It must devolve upon the family and the church. . . . It is enough to point out that the religious element of human culture is essential ; and that, by some effective agency, it must be presented to every child whose education aims at completeness or proportion.

What Knowledge is of Most Worth?

If it be true that spirit and reason rule the universe, then the highest and most enduring knowledge is of the things of the spirit. That subtile sense of the beautiful and the sublime which accompanies spiritual insight, and is part of it,—this is the highest achievement of which humanity is capable. It is typified, in various forms, in the verse of Dante and the prose of Thomas à Kempis, in the Sistine Madonna of Raphael, and in Mozart's Requiem. To develop this sense in education is the task of art and literature, to interpret it is the work of philosophy, and to nourish it the function of religion. Because it most fully represents the highest nature of man, it is man's highest possession, and those studies that directly appeal to it and instruct it are beyond compare the most valuable.

Properly interpreted, the study of nature may be classed among the humanities as truly as the study of language itself. . . . The study of nature is entitled to recognition on grounds similar to those put forward for the study of literature, of art, and of history.

In every field of knowledge which we are studying is some law or phase of energy, and the original as well as the highest energy is will. In the world of nature it is exhibited in one series of forms, those which produce the results known to us as chemical, physical, biological; in the history of mankind, it is manifested in the forms of feelings, thoughts, deeds, institutions. Because the elements of self-consciousness and reflection are present in the latter series and absent in the former, it is to these and the knowledge of them that we must accord the first place in any table of educational values.

Immediate utility makes demand upon the school which it is unable wholly to neglect.

There are utilities higher and utilities lower, and under no circumstances will the true

teacher ever permit the former to be sacrificed to the latter. This would be done if,
in its zeal for fitting the child for self-support,
the school were to neglect to lay the foundation for that higher intellectual and spiritual
life which constitutes humanity's full stature.
This foundation is made ready only if proper
emphasis be laid, from the kindergarten to
the college, on those studies whose subject-
matter is the direct product of intelligence
and will, and which can, therefore, make
direct appeal to man's higher nature.

Man's will gradually frees itself from
bondage to a chain of causes determined for
it from without, and attains to a power of
independent self-determination according to
durable and continuing ends of action. This
constitutes character, which, in Emerson's
fine phrase, is the moral order seen through
the medium of an individual nature.

While no knowledge is worthless,—for it
all leads us back to the common cause and
ground of all,—yet that knowledge is of
most worth which stands in closest relation

to the highest forms of the activity of that spirit which is created in the image of Him who holds nature and man alike in the hollow of His hand.

Is There a New Education?

There are three avenues of scientific approach to the study of education, and in each of them the evolutionary point of view is not only illuminating but controlling. These three avenues are the physiological, the psychological, and the new sociological.

The Greeks alone understood the educational value of play. Their great national games combined systematic physical training and play in a way that we have not yet succeeded in equalling. . . . In Germany systematic physical training is made much of in education, but genuine play is not prominent. In England, on the contrary, play has been found so successful in developing strength and suppleness of body and sturdy, independent character that anything approaching systematic, formal training is regarded as almost unnecessary. In this country the present tendency is to develop both elements.

But physical and physiological considerations cut far deeper than this. They demand a hearing when we have under discussion questions of school hours and recesses, of programmes and tasks, of school furniture, of textbooks and blackboards, of light, heat, and fresh air. . . . College faculties and school teachers, framers of examination tests, donors of laboratories and dormitories, and, most of all, architects, are, as a rule, oblivious to the vital interest that the pupil has in matters of this kind. Considerations of tradition, convenience, cost, and external appearance are allowed full swing, and the growing youth must fit the Procrustean bed as best they can.

We need to be strongly reminded that wickedness is closely akin to weakness, and then to consider the moral consequences of our physiological ignorance.

The relation of psychology to education is

the one subject on which the teacher of to-day is supposed to be informed. . . . Yet a careful inspection of the most popular text-books in use, and visits to some hundred classrooms, have convinced me that the results of this knowledge, if it exists, are, in the field of secondary and higher education, almost *nil.* In this respect the elementary teacher is far in advance.

They [teachers] are content to accumulate what they are pleased to term " experience " ; but their relation to education is just that of the motorman on a trolley-car to the science of electricity. They use it ; but of its nature, principles, and processes they are profoundly ignorant. The one qualification most to be feared in a teacher and the one to be most carefully inquired into, is this same " experience " when it stands alone. I am profoundly distrustful of it.

The pure empiricist never can have any genuine experience, any more than an animal, because he is unable to interrogate the phenomena that present themselves to him, and hence is unable to understand them. The scientific teacher, the theorist, on the contrary, asks what manner of phenomena these are that are before him, what are their inner relations, and the principles on which they are based.

This habit [of watching minds, and of watching them closely] is the surest road to good teaching, and its formation is the ˌbest service that psychology can render to the classroom. Until a teacher has acquired the habit and subordinated his schoolroom procedure to it, he is not teaching at all ; at best he is either lecturing or hearing recitations.

We are chiefly indebted to the students and followers of Herbart for the present wide-spread interest in this country in two psychological doctrines of the greatest importance for all teaching—the doctrine of apperception and the doctrine of interest. The former has to do with mental assimilation, the latter with the building of character and ideals.

The mind is not a passive recipient of the impressions that reach it; . . . . it reacts upon them, colors them, and makes them a part of itself in accordance with the tendency, the point of view, and the possessions that it already has. This tendency, this point of view, and these possessions differ in the case of every individual. Instead of over-looking or seeking to annul these differences, we should first understand them and base our teaching upon them.

I have known case after case in which the opposite policy of treating all upon one plane, and making the same demands upon all, has made a college course a source of positive harm.

The situation is not very different with respect to the doctrine of interest. . . . It is a common thing to hear it said that since life is full of obstacles and character is strengthened by overcoming them, so the school and college course should not hesi-tate to compel students to do distasteful and difficult things simply because they are distasteful and difficult. I do not hesitate to say that I believe that doctrine to be profoundly immoral and its consequences calamitous.

The proper and scientific course is to search for the pupil's empirical and natural interests, and to build upon them. This is not always easy; it requires knowledge, patience, and skill. It is far easier to treat the entire class alike.

I earnestly commend to every teacher the study of these two principles, apperception and interest. I do so in the firm belief that the practical result of that study would be an immense uplifting of the teaching efficiency of every educational institution in the United States.

What, for lack of a better term, I call the sociological aspect of education is, in many respects, the most important of all. . . . The first question to be asked of any course of study is, Does it lead to knowledge of our contemporary civilization? If not, it is neither efficient nor liberal.

In society as it exists to-day the dominant note, running through all our struggles and problems, is economic,—what the old Greeks might have called political. Yet it is a constant fight to get any proper teaching from the economic and social point of view put before high-school and college students.

We can leave questions as to the undulatory theory of light and as to Grimm's and Verner's laws to the specialists; but we may not do the same thing with questions as to production and exchange, as to monetary policy and taxation. The course of study is not liberal, in this century, that does not recognize these facts and emphasize economics as it deserves. I cite but this one instance of conflict between the inherited and the scientifically constructed course of study.

Dr. Johnson's acumen was equal to drawing a distinction between the new as the hitherto non-existent, the new as the comparatively recent, and the new as the hitherto unfamiliar. In each and all of these senses of the word, I am confident that there is a new education.

Democracy and Education.

Most striking and impressive of all movements of the century is the political development toward the form of government known as democracy. Steadily and doggedly throughout the ten decades the movement toward democracy has gone its conquering way.

So long as the direction of man's institutional life was in the hands of one or the few, the need for a wide diffusion of political intelligence was not strongly felt. The divine right of kings found its correlative in the diabolical ignorance of the masses. . . . But the rapid widening of the basis of sovereignty has changed all that. No deeper conviction pervades the people of the United States and of France, who are the most aggressive exponents of democracy, than that the preservation of liberty under the law, and of the institutions that are our precious possession and proud heritage, depends upon the intelligence of the whole people. It is on this unshakable foundation that the argument for public education at public expense really rests.

The teachers of the country should address themselves to this question with determination and zeal. Instruction in civil government is good ; the inculcation of patriotism is good ; the flag upon the school-house is good. But all these devices lie upon the surface. The real question involved is ethical. It reaches deep down to the very foundations of morality.

The public education of a great democratic people has other aims to fulfil than the extension of scientific knowledge or the development of literary culture. It must prepare for intelligent citizenship.

The good citizen is not the querulous critic of public men and public affairs, however intelligent he may be ; he is rather the constant participator in political struggles, who has well-grounded convictions and a strong determination to influence, by all honorable means, the opinion of the community. Were it otherwise, universal suffrage would not be worth having, and public education would be a luxury, not a necessity.

The spoils system is absolutely undemocratic and utterly unworthy of toleration by an intelligent people. . . . We teachers are the first to insist that incompetent and untrained persons shall not be allowed in the service of the schools. Why, then, should we tolerate the sight of a house-painter, instead of an engineer, supervising the streets and roadways of a city of a hundred thousand inhabitants, or that of an illiterate hanger-on presiding over the public works of a great metropolis? These instances, drawn at random from recent political history, are typical of conditions that will be found widely diffused throughout our public service.

The difficulties of democracy are the opportunities of education. If our education be sound, if it lay due emphasis on individual responsibility for social and political progress, if it counteract the anarchistic tendencies that grow out of selfishness and greed, if it promote a patriotism that reaches farther than militant jingoism and gunboats, then we may cease to have any doubts as to the perpetuity and integrity of our institutions.

I am profoundly convinced that the greatest educational need of our time, in higher and lower schools alike, is a fuller appreciation on the part of the teachers of what human institutions really mean and what tremendous moral issues and principles they involve.

College and University.

In order to become great—indeed, in order to exist at all—a university must represent the national life and minister to it.

With all its undisputed excellences, the

German system would not meet our needs
so well as the yet unsystematic, but remark-
ably effective, organization that circumstances have brought into existence.

But using the word [University] in a
broader, and, I believe, a truer sense,—the
sense that, while not confounding it with a
college, however large or however ancient,
nor applying it unmistakenly to a college
and a surrounding group of technical and
professional faculties or schools, yet extends
the term to include any institution where
students, *adequately trained by previous
study of the liberal arts and sciences*, are
led into special fields of learning and
research by teachers of high excellence and
originality; and where, by the agency of
libraries, museums, laboratories, and publica-
tions, knowledge is conserved, advanced, and
disseminated—in this sense one may perhaps count six or eight American universities in existence to-day, and half as many
more in the process of making.

Of the 481 American colleges, perhaps no two have precisely the same course of study or the same equipment ; but the common features that distinguish them are well known. . . . Wherever it is found, whether on the Atlantic seaboard, in some inland town of the West or South, or on the Pacific slope, the college is a force making for a broader intellectual life and a higher type of citizenship. It leaves to the university the task of educating specialists, investigators, and scientifically trained members of the learned professions.

The main obstacle to the full establishment in America of the pursuit of science for its own sake, as a controlling university principle, is the development and rapid growth of technical schools, with low standards of entrance, in connection with universities, and their admission to a full and even controlling share in university legislation and administration. Indeed, in this lies the chief danger to the integrity of American university development.

Whatever public opinion may rest satisfied with, it seems indisputable that universities owe it to themselves to put their
stamp upon no graduates in law, medicine,
and technology who are not liberally educated men.

What science and practical life alike need
is not narrow men, but broad men sharp-
ened to a point. To train such is the
highest function of the American university;
and by its success in producing them must
its efficiency be finally judged,

FROM "SCOPE AND FUNCTION OF
SECONDARY EDUCATION." [1]

What is secondary education? . . . .
The very name secondary implies that it has
reference to a primary or elementary education that comes before it. This elementary education I define as that general
training in the elements of knowledge that
is suitable for a pupil from the age of six or
seven to the period of adolescence. It is

---

[1] THE EDUCATIONAL REVIEW—June, 1898.

ordinarily organized in eight or nine grades each occupying an academic year. Nine grades are too many and are distinctly wasteful. . . . An eight-years' course is certainly ample for any community, and children should be given every encouragement and every opportunity to cover the elementary studies in even less time.

The marked characteristics of the pupil of secondary school age are due to the fact that, as Rousseau puts it, we are born twice : the first time into existence, the second time into life ; the first time as a member of the race, the second as a member of the sex—in other words, they are due to the phenomena of adolescence.

These facts point directly to the essential characteristics of secondary-school studies. They must, in the first place, be comparative and reflective in character in order to provide food for the newly discovered intellectual capacities ; in the second place, they must be and continue to become more and more difficult, in order to occupy and develop the augmented nervous and mental energy that now presents itself ; and in the third place, the tendency to introspection and analysis must be satisfied by the disclosing of the inner connections and deep reasons of the subjects taught.

Secondary studies make their appearance, and ought to make their appearance, in the upper grades of the elementary schools. The law of educational continuity demands this, and there is no other way to escape from the dreaded arrested development which falls like a pall upon so many of our school children.

As power is gained only by exercise, schoolmasters are beginning to find out that the quickest and surest way to lead pupils to the mastery of a given task is, after trying it a few times, not to review it indefinitely but to go forward to something more difficult. Good teaching will always keep a pupil's mind taut; to let it grow slack increases the friction and the waste.

Just as secondary studies take their rise

almost unnoticed among and out of the elementary studies, so they pass insensibly into those of college grade. The college point of view is more elevated, its scope broader, its methods still more reflective and abstract than those of the secondary school ; but no one can say dogmatically just where the one ends and the other begins.

Not the relative difficulty of studies, but their relations to each other, to the developing powers of the pupil, and to contemporary civilization, determine their order during the secondary and college periods.

The chief difficulty with secondary-school courses—and I am in the habit of studying scores of them every year—is that they include too many subjects pursued for too short a time. The horrible specter of " Fourteen Weeks," in this, that, or the other subject still haunts many schools, and an unintelligent ambition or a foolish local vanity contemplates it with ill-concealed satisfaction.

The dissipation of energy and the shattering of the highly coveted power of concentration that must follow any attempt to keep track of such an educational kaleidoscope, can better be imagined than described.

It is essential that studies should be organized in courses, and these courses may be as numerous and as diverse as the school can afford or as the community demands. These courses should not be rigid and compulsory: that involves another and hardly less serious danger.   They should be flexible and elective, made by each pupil for himself with the aid of his parents and teachers.

Each course should admit of attention to not more than five subjects at once, and each subject should be pursued long enough to gain such mastery of it as will cause it to yield to the student some considerable part of its educational value.

These flexible and elective courses. . . . must, of course, be organized about a common center or core. . . . The three constituent elements of this center or core, I state in this way: (1) the study of language: (2) the study of deductive reasoning, in mathematics and formal logic; (3) the study of inductive method, in experimental science and, in part, in history.

It is in this elimination of elementary studies from the secondary school and in the frank recognition of the paramount advantages of the elective system, that I see the way of highest usefulness opening before the secondary school. Instead of conducing to arrested development, it will then constantly spur the pupil on by putting new difficulties before him.

Mr. Herbert Spencer has told us that mankind, like a group of men selected at haphazard, is made up of a few clever individuals, many ordinary ones, and some decidedly stupid. The secondary school must recognize this fact, and not make the common mistake in trying to deal with a supposititious "average pupil": there is no average pupil.

During the secondary-school period, I repeat, tastes are to be developed into capacities and each pupil started on that line of interest and activity that is best adapted to him.

From "The Argument for Manual Training." [1]

The immediate end in all formal education is the development of the mind's powers and capacities. This end is always the same and is never absent. The means of education, on the other hand, are continually changing and depend upon two varying factors—our knowledge of the child's mind and the character of its environment. These two factors vary with the progress of knowledge, and are not quite the same in two consecutive decades, probably wholly different in two consecutive centuries.

Technical education is a training in some particular trade, industry, or set of trades or

[1] Teachers' Manuals, No. 11. New York and Chicago: E. L. Kellogg & Co., 1888.

industries, with a view to fitting the pupil to pursue it or them as the means of gaining a livelihood. It is a special education, like that of the lawyer or the physician. It takes for granted a general education and builds upon it as a foundation. Industrial education, on the other hand, is the foundation itself. It is the general and common training which underlies all instruction in particular techniques.

The manual training movement, as we know it, is new. It was put upon a strictly scientific basis a very short time ago indeed. But it has been "in the air," as the saying is, for a long time. Over two hundred and fifty years ago Comenius prescribed manual training as part of the true curriculum.

Froebel in his Kindergarten reduced theory to practice, and in the Kindergarten all manual training, as well as all rational and systematic education, has its basis.

Manual training is mental training through the hand and eye, just as the study of history is mental training through the memory and other powers.

Industrial education is a protest against this mental oligarchy, the rule of a few faculties. It is a demand for mental democracy, in which each power of mind, even the humblest, shall be permitted to occupy the place that is its due.

Too much stress cannot be laid upon the fact that manual training, as we use the term, is mental training. . . . What is it that models the graceful form and strikes the true blow, the muscles or the mind?[1] It is the mind that feels and fashions, and the mind that sees; the hand and the eye are the instruments which it uses.

It is not the business of the public school to turn out draughtsmen, or carpenters, or metal-workers, or cooks, or seamstresses, or modelers. Its aim is to send out boys and girls that are well and harmoniously trained

---

[1] Do the retina and optic nerves see, or does the mind?

to take their part in life. It is because manual training contributes to this end, that it is advocated.

For educational purposes we may agree that the mental powers are roughly divisible into two classes, the receptive and the expressive or active. By means of the former the child is put into possession of new facts, and by means of the second he makes these facts his own and uses them in practical life. As food will not nourish unless assimilated, so knowledge, or mental food, is not really knowledge, is not really possessed, until we have so gained control of it as to be able to express or use it.

Man can express his mental state or ideas by the use of language, by gesture, by delineation, and by construction. . . . The argument for manual training insists that each of these modes of expression must be considered, and that for the training of each a method must be devised.

It is essential in training both the powers

of reception and the powers of expression that the child deal with things and objects, and not alone with what some one has said or written about things.

Reading and writing are the only studies in the traditional group that train expression. . . . But even when well taught they are not adequate to the full demands of the mental powers of expression, for they rarely occupy more than ten per cent. of the school time, except in the very lowest primary grades.

The powers of expression by delineation and construction are trained by the reciprocal instruction in drawing and in constructive work. It is proved that the boy who can draw a cube, or he who can carve or mold one from wood or clay, knows more that is worth knowing about the cube than he who can merely repeat its geometrical definition.

Drawing lies at the basis of all manual training, and is to be taught in every grade as a means of expression of thought, only incidentally as an art.

Common-school education in the United States in these closing years of the nineteenth century . . . . demands that the observation, the judgment, and the executive faculty be trained at school as well as the memory and the reason. Despite the fact that the three former are the most important faculties that the human mind possesses, it is astounding how completely they are overlooked in the ordinary course of study.

We must bear in mind the growth of large cities and our unprecedented commercial and industrial development. . . . Indefinitely more people than ever before have to employ their observation, their judgment and their executive faculty, and employ them accurately, in the performance of their daily duties. For them, and through them, for all of us, the conditions of practical life have changed and are changing. Has the school responded to the new burdens thus laid upon it? The argument for manual training says no, it has not. A more comprehensive, a broader, a more practical training is necessary.

It is unquestionable that many of our social troubles originate in misunderstandings about labor and in false judgments as to what labor really is. . . . If manual training is accorded its proper place in education, if we come to see that manual work has in it a valuable disciplinary and educational element, our eyes will be opened as to its real dignity and men will cease to regard it as beneath them and their children. This is what I would call the social argument for manual training.

The economic argument is similar. It points out that the vast majority of our public-school children must earn their living with their hands, and therefore if the school can aid them in using their hands it is putting just so much bread and butter into their mouths.

I cordially indorse the pungent aphorism of Dr. Munger : " Education is to teach us how to live, not how to make a living." But while standing firmly on that platform, I do say that if the best and most complete edu-

cation happens to aid a boy in earning his
living that is no reason why it should be
supplanted by something less thorough and
less complete.

A movement at once so philosophic and
so far-reaching as that in favor of manual
training. . . . is the educational question of
the time.

The forces of conservatism are arrayed
against it as something new, and it is doubtless well that it is so, for education is altogether too important a matter to be swayed
by any and every crude theory.   Any new
movement to establish itself in education
must run a gauntlet of opposition and criticism, the safe passage of which is a guarantee
of excellence.   This gauntlet the manual-
training movement has successfully run, and
it is to-day the newest phase of educational
thought.

CHARLES WILLIAM ELIOT.

FROM "EDUCATIONAL REFORM." [1]

Inaugural Address :
As President of Harvard College.
October 19, 1869.

The endless controversies whether language, philosophy, mathematics or science supplies the best mental training, whether general education should be chiefly literary or chiefly scientific, have no practical lesson for us to-day. . . . we would have them all and at their best.

To observe keenly, to reason soundly, and to imagine vividly are operations as essential as that of clear and forcible expression ; and

[1] EDUCATIONAL REFORM: Essays and Addresses. CHARLES W. ELIOT. NewYork: THE CENTURY CO., 1898.

to develop one of these faculties it is not necessary to repress and dwarf the others.

Science no more than poetry finds its best warrant in its utility. Truth and right are above utility in all realms of truth and action.

The actual problem to be solved is not what to teach, but how to teach.

In education the individual traits of different minds have not been sufficiently attended to. Through all the period of boyhood the school studies should be representative ; all the main fields of knowledge should be entered upon. . . . When the revelation of his own peculiar taste and capacity comes to a young man, let him reverently give it welcome, thank God, and take courage.

The elective system fosters scholarship, because it gives free play to the natural preferences and inborn aptitudes, makes possible enthusiasm for a chosen work, relieves the professor and the ardent disciple of the presence of a body of students who are compelled to an unwelcome task, and enlarges instruction by substituting many and various lessons given to small, lively classes, for a few lessons many times repeated to different sections of a numerous class.

Both are useful—lectures, for inspiration, guidance, and the comprehensive methodizing which only one who has a view of the whole field can rightly contrive ; recitations, for securing and testifying a thorough mastery on the part of the pupil of the treatise or author in hand, for conversational comment and amplification, for emulation and competition.

In spite of the familiar picture of the moral dangers which environ the student, there is no place so safe as a good college during the critical passage from boyhood to manhood. . . . Its public opinion, though easily led astray, is still high in the main. Its scholarly tastes and habits, its eager friendships and quick hatreds, its keen debates, its frank discussions of character, and of deep political and religious questions, all are

safeguards against sloth, vulgarity, or de-
pravity. Its society and, not less, its soli-
tudes are full of teaching.

What is a Liberal Education?
1884.

Some of the studies now commonly called
liberal have not long held their preëmi-
nence; . . . . new learning has repeatedly
forced its way, in times past, to full academic
standing. . . . History teaches boldness in
urging the claims of modern literatures and
sciences to full recognition as liberal arts.

The first subject which, as I conceive, is
entitled to recognition as of equal academic
value or rank with any subject now most
honored is the English language and literature.

The next subjects for which I claim a
position of academic equality with Greek,
Latin, and Mathematics are French and
German. This claim rests. . . . on the mag-
nitude and worth of the literatures, and on
the unquestionable fact that facility in read-

ing these languages is absolutely indispensable to a scholar, whatever may be his department of study.

The next subject which demands an entirely different position from that it now occupies in American schools and colleges is history. If any study is liberal and liberalizing, it is the modern study of history—the study of the passions, opinions, beliefs, arts, laws, and institutions of different races or communities, and of the joys, sufferings, conflicts and achievements of mankind.

Closely allied to the study of history is the study of the new science called political economy, or public economics. . . . When we consider how formidable are the industrial, social, and political problems with which the next generation must grapple. . . . we can hardly fail to appreciate the importance of offering to large numbers of American students ample facilities for learning all that is known of economic science.

The last subject for which I claim admission to the magic circle of the liberal arts is natural science.

Natural science is to be studied not in books but in things. . . . The student of natural science scrutinizes, touches, weighs, measures, analyzes, dissects, and watches things. By these exercises his powers of observation and judgment are trained, and he acquires the precious habit of observing the appearances, transformations, and processes of nature. . . . He acquires the scientific method of study in the field. . . . the patient, cautious, sincere, self-directing spirit of natural science.

Since the beginning of this century they [the arts built upon chemistry, physics, botany, zoölogy, and geology] have wrought wonderful changes in the physical relation of man to the earth which he inhabits, in national demarcations, in industrial organization, in governmental functions, and in the modes of domestic life; and they will certainly do as much for the twentieth century as they have done for ours.

If the list of liberal arts is extended, as I have urged, it is manifest that no man can cover the whole ground and get a thorough knowledge of any subject. Hence the necessity of allowing the student to choose among many co ördinate studies the few to which he will devote himself.

It is a waste for society, and an outrage upon the individual, to make a boy spend the years when he is most teachable in a discipline the end of which he can never reach, when he might have spent them in a different discipline, which would have been rewarded by achievement. Herein lies the fundamental reason for options among school as well as college studies, all of which are liberal.

A mental discipline which takes no account of differences of capacity and taste is not well directed. It follows that there must be variety in education instead of uniform prescription.

Liberty in Education.
1885.

A university of liberal arts and sciences must give its students three things :

I. Freedom in choice of studies. . . . The individual enjoys most that intellectual labor for which he is the most fit ; and society is best served when every man's peculiar skill, faculty, or aptitude is developed and utilized to the highest possible degree.

There exist certain natural guides and safeguards for every youth who is called upon in a free university to choose his own studies. . . . He cannot avoid taking up a subject which he has already studied about where he left off, and every new subject at the beginning and not in the middle. . . . Every advanced course, whether in language, philosophy, history, mathematics, or science, presupposes acquaintance with some elementary course or courses. . . . There is a prevailing tendency on the part of every competent student to carry far any congenial subject once entered upon. . . . So effective are these natural safeguards against fickleness and inconsecutiveness in the choice of studies that artificial regulation is superfluous.

I have never known a student of any capacity to select for himself a set of studies covering four years which did not apparently possess more theoretical and practical merit for his case than the required curriculum of my college days.

But what becomes, under such a system, of the careless, indifferent, lazy boys who have no bent or intellectual ambition of any sort? . . . . What becomes of such boys under the uniform compulsory system? . . . . It really does not make much difference what these unawakened minds dawdle with. There is, however, much more chance that such young men will get roused from their lethargy under an elective system than under a required.

II. A university must give its students opportunity to win distinction in special subjects or lines of study. The uniform curriculum led to a uniform degree, the first scholar and the last receiving the same diploma. A university. . . . must provide academic honors at graduation for distinguished attainments in single subjects.

III. A university must permit its students, in the main, to govern themselves. . . . It is not the business of a university to train men for those functions in which implicit obedience is of the first importance. On the contrary, it should train men for those occupations in which self-government, independence, and originating power are pre ëminently needed.

Such a university is the safest place in the world for young men who have anything in them. . . . The student lives in a bracing atmosphere ; books engage him ; good companionships invite him ; good occupations defend him ; helpful friends surround him ; pure ideals are held up before him ; ambition spurs him ; honor beckons him.

Can School Programmes be Shortened and Enriched? 1888.

The subject seems to be one chiefly interesting to colleges [as relating to earlier college entrance] but really has a much broader scope. . . . Whatever improves the school programmes for those children whose education is to be prolonged, perhaps, until they are twenty-five years old, will improve the programmes also for the less fortunate children whose education is to be briefer.

In the first place, better programmes need better teachers.

The American schools will never equal the schools of Germany and France until well-proved teachers can secure a tenure during good behavior and efficiency, like teachers in those countries.

The average skill of the teachers in the public schools may be increased by raising the present low proportion of male teachers in the schools. . . . This superiority of men

as teachers has, of course, nothing to do with
the relative intelligence and faithfulness of
men and women. . . . Many women enter
the public schools as teachers without any
intention of long following the business ; and
also. . . . women are absent from duty from
two to three times as much as men. . . .
The schools need the life-work of highly
trained and experienced teachers.

Cheap teachers and expensive apparatus
and buildings are precisely the reverse of
wise practice.

As a rule the American programmes do
not seem to be substantial enough, from the
first year in the primary school onward.
There is not enough meat in the diet. They
do not bring the child forward fast enough
to maintain his interest, and induce him to
put forth his strength.

It is not work which causes overfatigue so
much as lack of interest and lack of conscious progress. . . . One problem in arith-

metic which he cannot solve will try a child more than ten he can solve.

American teaching in school and college has been chiefly driving and judging ; it ought to be leading and inspiring.

Much time can be saved in primary and secondary schools by diminishing the number of reviews, and by never aiming at the kind of accuracy of attainment which reviews, followed by examinations, are intended to enforce.

Instead of mastering one subject before going to another, it is almost invariably wise to go on to a superior subject before the inferior has been mastered—mastery being a very rare thing. On the mastery theory, how much new reading or thinking should we adults do ?

The really profitable time to review a subject is not when we have just finished it, but when we have used it in studying other subjects, and have seen its relation to other subjects and what it is good for.

The French programme puts a review of arithmetic, algebra, and geometry into the last year. With all his mathematical powers strengthened by the study of algebra and geometry and with all the practice of arithmetic which his study of mensuration and algebra has involved, the boy returns at seventeen to arithmetic and finds it infinitely easier than he did at fourteen. Further, the French boy has escaped those most exasperating of arithmetical puzzles which a little easy algebra enables one to solve with facility.

It is one of the worst defects of examinations that they set an artificial value upon accuracy of attainment.

In all the numerous collections of school statistics in this country, it appears that the various grades contain children much too old for them, who have apparently been held back. . . . The result of this retardation is that the boy comes too late to the high school or the Latin school, and so fails to complete that higher course if he is going on to business, or comes too late to college if his education is to be more prolonged.

The great body of children ought to pass regularly from one grade to another, without delay, at the ages set down on the programme ; and any method of examination which interferes with this regular progress does more harm than good.

The Gap Between Common Schools and Colleges. 1890.

To improve secondary education in the United States, two things are necessary : (1) more schools are needed ; (2) the existing schools need to be brought to common and higher standards, so that the colleges may find in the school courses a firm, broad, and reasonably homogeneous foundation for their higher work.

The Aims of the Higher Education. 1891.

Many people draw a distinction between

an educated and a practical man ; but true education is, after all, nothing but systematic study and practice under guidance.

Universities have three principal direct functions. In the first place they teach ; secondly, they accumulate great stores of acquired and systematized knowledge in the form of books and collections ; thirdly, they investigate, or, in other words, they seek to push out a little beyond the present limits of knowledge, and learn, year by year, day after day, some new truth. They are teachers, storehouses, and searchers for truth.

A great university exerts a unifying social influence. . . . The whole organization of college life is intensely democratic, and there is a complete fusion of the whole body of students in all the intellectual and all the athletic pursuits of the place.

In a true university the differences between the various religious denominations are softened, and mutual respect between these diverse Christian organizations is cultivated. . . . In such institutions great bodies of American youth acquire a respect for each other's religious inheritances, and learn that conduct has very little to do with creed, or at least is not dependent upon theological opinion.

A university has a unifying influence by its effect upon political divisions. . . . There is. . . . a continual ferment and agitation on all questions of public interest. This collision of views is wholesome and profitable ; it promotes thought on great themes ; converts passion into resolution, cultivates forbearance and mutual respect, and teaches young men to admire candor, moral courage, and independence of thought on whatever side these noble qualities may be displayed.

A university of national resort exerts a unifying influence through the mutual knowledge which the young men get of one another and hold through life.

American universities are schools of pub-

lic spirit for the communities in which they
are situated.   They promote thought and
labor for the public on the part of private
persons in two ways : first by demanding a
great deal of gratuitous service from their
trustees, or managers ; and secondly, by
encouraging private benefactions for public
objects.

A university stands for spiritual and intellectual domination—for the forces of the
mind and soul against the overwhelming
load of material possessions, interests and
activities, which the modern world carries.

A university is in all countries a patriotic
institution. . . .   They seek ideals, and our
country in the modern sense is one of the
noblest of ideals, being no longer represented
by an idealized person, as the king or queen,
but being rather a personified ideal, free,
strong and beautiful.

Are all these aims of the higher education
anywhere attained ?   Nowhere, as yet.   But

they surely will be as our republic grows in wealth, wisdom and true worth.

The Grammar-School Course. 1892.

Averaging the rates of progress of bright children with those of dull children being the great curse of a graded school, it is safer to make the regular programme for eight grades, and lengthen it for the exceptionally slow pupils, than to make it for ten grades, and shorten it for the exceptionally quick. . . . Holding back the capable children is a much greater injustice than hurrying the incapable.

The first great reduction [in the volume and variety of the present studies] should, I believe, be made in arithmetic. . . . On grounds of utility, geometry and physics have stronger claims than any part of arithmetic beyond the elements, and for mental training they are also to be preferred. . . . They have proved to be interesting and intelligible to American children from eleven to thirteen years of age. . . . Moreover, the

attainments of the pupils in arithmetic are
not diminished by the introduction of the
new studies, but rather increased.

Secondly, language studies, including
reading, writing, spelling, grammar and
literature, occupy from one-third to two-
fifths of most grade programmes. There is
ample room here for the introduction of the
optional study of a foreign language, ancient
or modern, at the fourth or fifth grade.

Thirdly. . . . by grouping physical geography with natural history, and political
geography with history, and by providing
proper apparatus for teaching geography,
time can be saved, and yet a place made
for much new and interesting geographical
instruction.

[Noting objections to these changes, President Eliot observes :]
Practice in thinking with accuracy and
working with demonstrable precision can be
obtained in algebra, geometry, and physics
just as well as in arithmetic. It is quite un-

necessary to adhere to the lowest and least interesting of these exact subjects in order to secure adequate practice in precision of thought and work.

It is a curious fact that we Americans habitually underestimate the capacity of pupils at almost every stage of education, from the primary school through the university. . . . It seems to me probable that the proportion of grammar-school children incapable of pursuing geometry, algebra, and foreign language would turn out to be much smaller than we now imagine ; but though their proportion should be large, it would not justify the exclusion of all the capable children from opportunities which they could profit by.

The changes proposed. . . . are really essential to a truly democratic school system ; for they must be adopted and carried into effect before the children of the poor can obtain equal access with the children of the rich to the best education they are capable of, whatever the grade of that education may be. . . . The rich man can obtain for his children a suitably varied course of instruction, with much individual teaching, in a private or endowed school; but the immense majority of American children are confined to the limited uniform machine programme of the graded grammar-school. A democratic society was never more misled as to its own interest than in supposing such a programme to be for the interest of the masses.

[These changes] are indeed for the interest of this class of children [whose education is to be carried beyond the grammar-school to the high school and possibly to the college]; but they are much more for the interest of the children who are not going to the high school, and for whom, therefore, the grammar-school is to provide all the systematic education they will ever receive.

There are two effective precautions against the ill effects attributed to overwork at school—precautions which, it is delightful to see, are more and more adopted. They are good ventilation and the systematic use of light gymnastics at regular intervals during school hours.

There is, however, a third precaution against overwork which is quite as important as either of these already mentioned ; it is making school work interesting to the children. . . . To introduce new and higher subjects into the school programme is not necessarily to increase the strain upon the child. If this measure increases the interest and attractiveness of the work and the sense of achievement, it will diminish weariness and the risk of hurtful strain.

Parents are sensitive about the promotion of their children. They want the dull ones and the bright to be promoted at the same rate. . . . In Harvard College, where there is no such thing as a uniform programme of study for all students, ... we have long abandoned uniform attainment as ground of promotion. The sole ground of promotion is reasonable fidelity. I venture to believe that this is the true ground of promotion in grammar-schools as well.

I see many evidences that a great and beneficent change in public-school pro-grammes is rapidly advancing. The best evidence is to be found in the keen interest which superintendents and teachers take in the discussion of the subject.

The Grammar-School of the Future. 1893.

These are necessary conditions for health-ful mental activity: good air, good light, and, every hour or two, out-of-door exercise. I believe the grammar-school of the future will have about it a large open piece of ground.

The grammar-school of the future is to have a large assortment of apparatus of vari-ous kinds. To begin with, it will have books. . . . We realize that every subject needs to be illustrated, for both teacher and pupil, by many and various books.

There is no subject that does not require

its apparatus for teaching [e. g., Chemistry ; Physics ; Geometry].

It is extraordinary what interest and train-ing-power are imparted to Geography, sim-ply by the addition of one means of illustra-tion, namely, photographs of scenery. There is no point in reference to the formation of plains and plateaus, of mountains and valleys, of lakes and rivers, which cannot be beauti-fully illustrated by photographs. I say, therefore, that the grammar-school of the future will have within its walls a large as-sortment of models, charts, maps, globes, and photographs, for the teaching of Geogra-phy.

This, again, means the expenditure of money. And how can we hope to acquire for the grammar-school these costly materi-als? . . . . All these things can be gradually added with a moderate annual expenditure . . . . and the tendency of recent years is to decrease their cost.

Another matter. . . . we are apt to find

from fifty to sixty children under the charge of a single teacher —ordinarily a young girl whose experience in teaching has been short and will be short. . . . Never have I seen a university teacher trying to deal five hours a day with as many pupils as are put before every young grammar-school teacher in the city of Boston, for example. . . . and these . . . . are men of high training, large experience, and great earnestness. It is obvious that the young woman with fifty or sixty pupils before her is attempting what no mortal can perform.

The new teaching. . . . requires alertness, vitality, and sympathetic enthusiasm. It is exhausting. Virtue goes out of the teacher at every moment.

What is the possible remedy ? To double the number of teachers would not be too much. . . . The individual requires teaching in these days, and no teaching is good which does not pay attention to the individual. . . . But we must admit that to double the number of teachers is not a practical aim, at

present, whether in the city or in the country. We ask, therefore, is there no other
possible solution of this serious difficulty?

At Harvard University. . . . the professor can set before a whole class in an hour
an outline of a course of study that will occupy them a month. . . . He can fill them,
if he has it in him, with the enthusiasm
which is to carry them on for a whole month.
. . . . But when it comes to supervision of
the daily work of a large number of students
. . . . we provide assistants. . . . young
graduates who have been through these
very courses, generally under the guidance
of the same professor whom they assist.
They meet the principal teacher weekly or
daily, and get their entire guidance from
him. . . . I am not prepared to say that
the selection of the assistants by any other
than the leading teacher would work well.

One other suggestion. . . . is that the
principal teachers in any urban school system, and superintendents in any school sys-

tem, urban or rural, should take the part of the professor leading a class. I believe that the schools need many more highly-trained and experienced teachers than they now have, and that these principal teachers can work advantageously in many schools on the departmental plan.

The Conferences on Secondary Education which met last December recommended a great extension of the subjects which are used in the grammar-schools of to-day, and the correlation of those subjects in teaching. so that all teachers may take an interest in several subjects. This recommendation would bring into the grammar-school many subjects now belonging to the high school ; and this change would cause the greatest possible improvement in the grammar-school of the future.

In a democracy the public schools should enable any child to get the best training possible up to any year, not for the humblest destinations only, but for all destinations. This is the true view of the grammar-schools.

The American grammar-school will make that the rule which is now the exception — every child without special favor to get at the right subject at the right age, and to pursue it just as far and as fast as he is able to travel.

The American people accept, as one just definition of democracy, Napoleon's phrase, " Every career open to talent " ; and I believe that this saying will fairly characterize the grammar-school of the future.

The Unity of Educational Reform. 1894.

The chief principles and objects of modern educational reform are quite the same from beginning to end of that long course of education which extends from the fifth or sixth to the twenty-fifth or twenty-sixth year of life. The phrase " educational construction " would perhaps be better than the phrase " educational reform " ; for in our day and country we are really constructing all the methods of universal democratic education.

The first of these objects is the promotion of individual instruction.

Secondly, let me ask your attention to six essential constituents of all worthy education. . . . The careful training of the organs of sense. . . . Practice in grouping and comparing different sensations or contacts, and in drawing inferences from such comparisons. . . . Training in making a record of the observation, the comparison, or the grouping. . . . Training of the memory. . . . Training in the power of expression. . . . The steady inculcation of. . . . the ideals of beauty, honor, duty, and love.

Effective power in action is the true end of education, rather than the storing up of information, or the cultivation of faculties which are mainly receptive, discriminating, or critical.

The selection or election of studies. . . . has been adopted by all colleges or universities worthy of the name, and by the greater part of the leading high schools, academies,

endowed schools, and private schools. . . .
It has within a few years penetrated the
grades of the grammar-schools, and has
earned its way to a frank recognition at that
stage of education.

By preference, permanent motives [for dis-
cipline] should be relied on from beginning
to end of education. . . . The formation of
habits is a great part of education, and in
that formation of habits is inextricably involved the play of those recurrent emotions,
sentiments, and passions which lead to habi-
tual volitions. Among the permanent
motives which act all through life are pru-
dence, caution, emulation, love of approbation,—and particularly the approbation of
persons respected or beloved,—shame, pride,
self-respect, pleasure in discovery, activity
or achievement, delight in beauty, strength,
grace and grandeur, and the love of power,
and of possessions as giving power. Any of
these motives may be over-developed ; but
in moderation they are all good, and they
are available from infancy to old age.

The specialization of instruction is a common need from beginning to end of any rational system of instruction, and . . . . it is capable of adding indefinitely to the dignity, pleasure and serviceableness of the teacher's life.

Administrative officers in educational institutions should be experts, and not amateurs or emigrants from other professions, and. . . .teachers should have large advisory functions in the administration of both schools and universities.

The Function of Education in Democratic Society. October, 1897.

Democratic education being a very new thing in the world, its attainable objects are not yet fully perceived.

As soon as the easy use of what I have called the tools of education [reading, writing, and simple ciphering] is acquired, and even while this familiarity is being gained, the capacity for productiveness and enjoyment should begin to be trained through the progressive acquisition of an elementary knowledge of the external world. The democratic school should begin early—in the very first grades—the study of nature.

The process of making acquaintance with external nature through the elements of the various sciences [physical geography, meteorology, botany, zoölogy, chemistry, physics, geometry] should be interesting and enjoyable for the child. It should not be painful, but delightful.

The study of the human race should be gradually conveyed to the child's mind from the time he begins to read with pleasure. This study should be conveyed quite as much through biography as through history; and, with the descriptions of facts and real events, charming and uplifting products of the imagination.

Organized education must. . . . supply in urban communities a good part of the manual and moral training which the coöperation of children in the work of father and mother affords in agricultural communities.

The school should teach every child, by precept, by example and by every illustration its reading can supply, that the supreme attainment for any individual is vigor and loveliness of character.

From the total training during childhood then should result in the child a taste for interesting and improving reading, which should direct and inspire its subsequent intellectual life. . . . The uplifting of the democratic masses depends on this implanting at school of the taste for good reading.

Another important function of the public school in a democracy is the discovery and development of the gift or capacity of each individual child. . . . It is one of the main advantages of fluent and mobile democratic society that it is more likely than any other society to secure the fruition of individual capacities. . . . In the ideal democratic school no two children would follow the same course of study or have the same tasks, except that they would all need to learn the use of the elementary tools of education—reading, writing, and ciphering.

Certain habits of thought should be well established in the minds of all the children before any of them are obliged to leave school in order to help in the support of the family. In some small field each child should acquire a capacity for exact observation . . . . for exact description . . . . and the power to draw a justly limited inference from observed facts.

Any one who has attained to the capacity for exact observation and exact description, and knows what it is to draw a correct inference from well-determined premises, will naturally acquire a respect for those powers when exhibited by others in fields unknown to him. . . . He will be sure that the too common belief that a Yankee can turn his hand to anything is a mischievous delusion. . . . In short, he will come to respect and confide in the expert in every field of human activity. . . . and in any democracy which is to thrive, this respect and conficence must be felt strongly by a majority of the population.

Democracies will not be safe until the population has learned that governmental affairs must be conducted on the same principle on which success for private and corporate business is conducted.

The next function. . . . should be the firm planting in every child's mind of certain great truths which lie at the foundation of the democratic social themes. . . . the intimate dependence of each human individual on a multitude of other individuals—not in infancy alone, but at every moment of life [in present living and in the debt owed to former generations]. . . . the essential unity of a democratic community, in spite of the endless diversities of function, capacity, and achievement. . . . the familiar Christian doctrine that service rendered to others is the sweet source of one's own satisfaction and happiness.

Finally, the democratic school must teach

its children what the democratic nobility is. . . . Fidelity to all forms of duty which demand courage, self-denial and zeal, and loyal devotion to the democratic ideals of freedom, serviceableness, unity, toleration, public justice, and public joyfulness.

THE "NUGGETS" SERIES

"DON'T WORRY" NUGGETS: From Epictetus, Emerson, George Eliot, Robert Browning. Gathered by Jeanne G. Pennington. *Portrait of Emerson.*

PATRIOTIC NUGGETS: From Franklin, Washington, Jefferson, Webster, Lincoln, Beecher. Gathered by John R. Howard. *Portrait of Washington.*

EDUCATIONAL NUGGETS: From Plato, Aristotle, Rousseau, Herbart, Harris, Butler, Eliot. Gathered by John R. Howard. *Portrait of Plato.*

PHILOSOPHIC NUGGETS: From Carlyle, Ruskin, Charles Kingsley, Amiel. Gathered by Jeanne G. Pennington. *Portrait of Carlyle.*

Uniform size and style: 3⅜ by 5⅜ : *Flexible cloth, gilt top:* **40 cents.**

FORDS, HOWARD, & HULBERT
47 East Tenth St., New York